TOUR OF MONTE ROSA

© Tracey Fantham

About the Author

Hilary Sharp is British and holds the International Mountain Leader diploma. After 23 years based in the French alpine village of Vallorcine near Chamonix Mont Blanc, she has now relocated further south to the warmer climes of Provence. She runs her own trekking business, Trekking in the Alps and Provence, guiding walks in winter, spring and summer (hilaryalp@gmail.com, www.trekkinginthealps.com, www.trekkinginprovence.com). Her love of walking and climbing has taken her to many parts of Europe and further afield.

Hilary contributes to several British walking magazines and is author of *Trekking and Climbing in the Western Alps* (New Holland, 2002, out of print). She is also a keen outdoor photographer.

Other Cicerone guides by the author
Snowshoeing: Mont Blanc and the Western Alps
Mont Blanc Walks
Tour of the Matterhorn
Chamonix Mountain Adventures

TOUR OF MONTE ROSA

by Hilary Sharp

2 POLICE SQUARE, MILNTHORPE, CUMBRIA LA7 7PY
www.cicerone.co.uk

© Hilary Sharp 2015

Second edition 2015
ISBN: 978 1 85284 730 2
First edition 2007
ISBN: 978 1 85284 454 7

A catalogue record for this book is available from the British Library.

Acknowledgements

Lots of people helped me with the first edition of this book, notably Jean-Luc Lugon and Alberto Calaba, owner of the now defunct Rifugio Guglielmina. For this revision I am indebted to Anna Pagani, guardian of the Rifugio Pastore for her ever cheerful replies to my questions. I also want to thank all those people who trek with me and enhance my photos – I am lucky to have such willing and photogenic models. Finally, thanks are due to my husband Jon de Montjoye who once again was in charge of the maps and helped with research.

Updates to this Guide

While every effort is made by our authors to ensure the accuracy of guidebooks as they go to print, changes can occur during the lifetime of an edition. Any updates that we know of for this guide will be on the Cicerone website (www.cicerone.co.uk/730/updates), so please check before planning your trip. We also advise that you check information about such things as transport, accommodation and shops locally. Even rights of way can be altered over time. We are always grateful for information about any discrepancies between a guidebook and the facts on the ground, sent by email to info@cicerone.co.uk or by post to Cicerone, 2 Police Square, Milnthorpe LA7 7PY, United Kingdom.

Front cover: Stunning views of the East Face of Monte Rosa from the Rifugio Oberto Maroli, just below the Monte Moro Pass (Stage 6)

CONTENTS

Map Key

～～～	ridge		
≈≈≈	road		
～～～	main route		
⌒⌒	variant (described)		
～～～	variant (mentioned)		
∿∿∿	difficult section (sometimes equipped with cables)		
∿∿∿	glacier section		
━ ∙ ━ ∙ ━	national boundary		
～～～	river		
▭	lake	⋈	col
▱	glacier	▲	summit
├───┤	cable way	■	habitation
┼┼┼┼┼┼	railway	♱	church/chapel
⬆	mountain hut	＝	bridge
━	dam		

Mountain Safety

Every mountain walk has its dangers, and those described in this guidebook are no exception. All who walk or climb in the mountains should recognise this and take responsibility for themselves and their companions along the way. The author and publisher have made every effort to ensure that the information contained in this guide was correct when it went to press, but they cannot accept responsibility for any loss, injury or inconvenience sustained by any person using this book.

International Distress Signal *(emergency only)*
Six blasts on a whistle (and flashes with a torch after dark) spaced evenly for one minute, followed by a minute's pause. Repeat until an answer is received. The response is three signals per minute followed by a minute's pause.

Helicopter Rescue
The following signals are used to communicate with a helicopter:

Help needed:
raise both arms
above head to
form a 'Y'

Help not needed:
raise one arm
above head, extend
other arm downward

Emergency telephone numbers
In all EU countries 112 is the emergency phone number (landline and mobile)
Italy: Police (and general emergency) ☎ 113;
Carabinieri (military police) ☎ 112;
Medical emergency and rescue ☎ 118; Fire or disaster ☎ 115
Switzerland: Fire ☎ 118; Police ☎ 117; Medical and rescue ☎ 144;
Helicopter air rescue (Rega) ☎ 1414 or 144, or radio 161.300MHz

Weather reports
(If telephoning from the UK the dialling codes are:
France: 0033; Italy: 0039; Switzerland: 0041)

France: www.meteo.fr or ☎ 3250
Italy: ☎ 0165 44 113
Switzerland: ☎ 162 (in French, German or Italian), www.meteoschweiz.ch/en

Note Mountain rescue can be very expensive – be adequately insured.

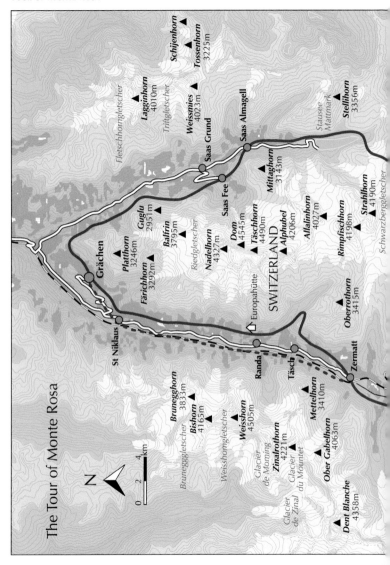

The Tour of Monte Rosa

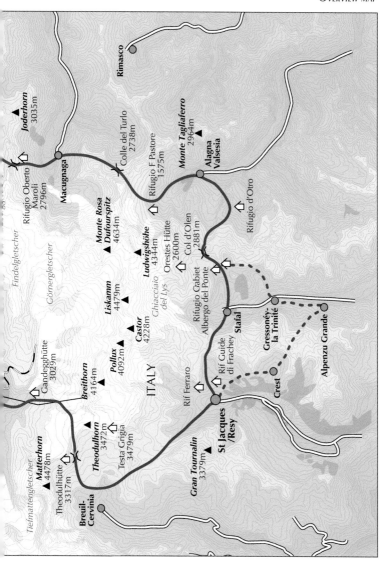

The Nordend summit of Monte Rosa

INTRODUCTION

The Monte Rosa massif has inspired not only mountaineers but also poets, writers, visitors and explorers for generations. This mountain range is a visual bastion, dominating viewpoints from valleys on all sides. As Leonardo da Vinci wrote in his Milanese memoirs at the end of the 15th century, the Monte Rosa 'is so high that it seems almost to overtake the clouds'.

The Tour of Monte Rosa is a journey of dreams, an adventure that goes way beyond a hike or trek, a voyage of discovery in one of the most fascinating Alpine regions. To treat it as a mere walking tour would be to miss out on so much: the varied culture of the Swiss and Italian valleys and mountain villages; the gastronomic specialities which change from one valley to the next; the people encountered; the rich history of the area; the wealth and diversity of plant life and animals.

This is a trek to be savoured. If you do not have time to complete it in a leisurely fashion you may be well advised to do a section one year and leave the rest for another visit, rather than miss out on the chance to immerse yourself fully in the experience.

Monte Rosa is far from being a single summit. This is the biggest

A great view of Monte Rosa from the Rifugio Oberto Maroli on Stage 6

massif in Western Europe, comprising ten defined summits which surpass the magical 4000m mark. Although now surrounded on all sides by resorts and mechanical uplift, the ascent of the Monte Rosa peaks remains a challenging undertaking, not to be underestimated. Winter and summer alike, the nearby slopes are home to skiers and tourists, but to reach a Monte Rosa summit you need to be fit and acclimatised. All around are glaciers, seracs and crevasses, and although in good sunny conditions deep snow tracks lead to the summits and give a sense of security, as soon as the fog comes down or the snow starts to fall this area becomes a very serious proposition indeed.

To walk around the Monte Rosa massif is to enjoy all the views and the incredible scenery with none of the dangers and perils associated with ascending the peaks. The Tour flirts just a little with the glaciers as it passes from Italy to Switzerland via the Theodulpass, leading the hiker into the high mountain world of ice and snow. But there are far more demanding ascents than this one on the Tour.

Apart from that short glaciated section this is a trek on non-glaciated ground. It is a wonderful route that climbs up from the valley bases through meadows, past summer farms and grazing cows, onto the higher rocky slopes where only the hardiest animals live, and over passes tucked up against the slopes of glaciated mountains, then descending new valleys, each different in character and scenery.

THE REGION

The Monte Rosa massif forms part of the Pennine Alps (a mountain range in the western part of the Alps), and borders southern Switzerland and northern Italy. The Pennine Alps are located in France (Haute-Savoie), Switzerland (Valais) and Italy (Piedmont and Valle d'Aosta). The Petit Saint Bernard Pass and the Dora Baltea Valley separate them from the Graian Alps; the

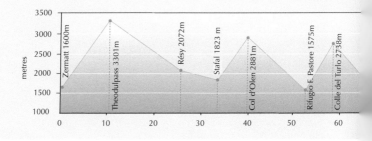

The fabulously blue Gran Lago passed on Stage 2

Simplon Pass separates them from the Lepontine Alps; the Rhône Valley separates them from the Bernese Alps; and the Col de Coux and the Arly Valley separate them from the French Prealps (Aravis and Chablais). The Pennine Alps contain the largest concentration of peaks over 4000m in Europe. The Swiss-Italian frontier forms the Alpine watershed and it is here that the most grandiose summits are to be found, their huge glaciers snaking down into the adjacent valleys: on the Swiss side flowing down

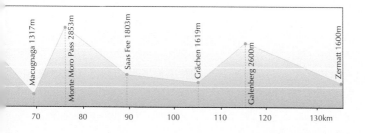

13

to the Rhône, on the Italian draining to the Po.

The enormous barrier of the Pennine Alps represents the pressure zone created when the African tectonic plate collided with the Continental plate. Mountains were forced up and subsequent erosion has produced the spectacular scenery seen today. While very slightly less lofty than their famous neighbour Mont Blanc, peaks such as Liskamm, the ten summits of Monte Rosa, the Täschhorn, the Dom and the Weisshorn, to mention just a few, are at least equal in grandeur and splendour.

The Tour of Monte Rosa visits two countries, Italy and Switzerland. These are mountain regions, initially inhabited by people who probably arrived from other mountain valleys. To some extent cut off from life down on the plains, these regions have maintained their traditions and culture. Life was naturally harsh, especially during the long winter months. A common thread runs through the villages and valleys encountered on the trek – that of sustainable living – surviving on whatever you have locally.

The Italian regions are the Valle d'Aosta and Piedmont. A close look at a map will reveal that although it is only a day's walk to get over from Switzerland to Macugnaga or Alagna, for example, it's a very long drive from the main Italian valleys. This relative inaccessibility gives unique character to these remote Alpine villages.

On the Italian side the trek passes through some villages incorporating a Walser settlement. These people have Germanic origins, their ancestors having made the journey to the mountains around AD1000. They settled in many Alpine regions, notably around Alagna and Macugnaga, and still preserve the basics of their original culture.

The Swiss part of the trek is exclusively in the Wallis canton, staying high above the Saas and Matter valleys. The relatively new Europaweg (established 2000) links with the long-existing Höhenweg to make the world's longest balcony path (at least that's how it feels) all the way from Saas Fee to Zermatt. While this trail is a visual joy, it does keep the hiker away from some of the charming villages in the valley – it may be that the future Tour of Monte Rosa takes to the valley paths (shown as Stage 8A in this guide) to avoid the Europaweg, which has serious maintenance problems, and the upside of this will be the chance to discover these traditional hamlets. Zermatt and Saas Fee – along with Grächen, which sits between these high-traversing trails – provide a good insight into life in this German-speaking part of Switzerland.

THE MONTE ROSA MASSIF

When driving up from the lowlands of the Po Valley past Milan on a clear day you will notice a misty mass rearing up in the distance. Soon you will

Monte Rosa's four highest summits (L to R): Nordend, Dufourspitze, Zumsteinspitze and Signalkuppe with the Margherita Hut just visible close to its 4559m summit

distinguish snowy slopes and rocky buttresses, but even so this huge massif seems completely improbable from the motorway. This is the Monte Rosa massif, and you will better understand its situation and associated culture and weather if you can visualise its exact location. The massif forms the southern extremity of the Pennine Alps, and is the first obstacle encountered when heading up from the southern plains. The massif is shared between Switzerland and Italy, situated in the Italian regions of Piedmont (provinces of Verbania and of Vercelli) and the Valle d'Aosta (province of Aosta), and the Swiss canton of Valais (Wallis). The name *pied monte* literally means 'at the foot of the mountains'.

Facts and figures

The Monte Rosa massif is very large – the biggest in the Alps – with 22 peaks over 4000m. Ten of these peaks form Monte Rosa itself. The high point of Monte Rosa is the Dufourspitze, which at 4634m is the second-highest peak in the Western Alps. The official limits of the Monte Rosa massif are:

- **West** Theodulpass (3317m)
- **East** Monte Moro Pass (2853m)
- **North** Schwarzberg-Weisstor, next to the Rimpfischhorn, in the Mischabelgruppe (4199m)
- **South** Col d'Olen (2881m).

Matters are made more complicated by the fact that the massif straddles the Swiss-Italian frontier and thus many of the summits have both Italian and Swiss names (and sometimes different altitudes as the maps do not always concur!).

The northern side belongs to Switzerland and holds the greatest glaciers, such the Gorner Glacier (Gornergletscher), which is the second-largest glacier in the Alps and runs down to the Zermatt Valley (Mattertal). The Italian side is far less glaciated since it faces south and east, and here the most important is the Lys Glacier (Ghiacciaio del Lys or Ghiacciaio di Gressoney).

One of the most fascinating aspects of the Monte Rosa is its East Face, which is the highest in the Alps. There is a height difference of around 2470m between the meadows at the end of Valle Anzasca to the top of the mountain. Seen from Macugnaga, the face forms a steep and colossal barrier – virtually a Himalayan wall in the Alps. It features one of the longest couloirs of the Alps, known as the Canalone Marinelli after its first ascentionists. Also in the Monte Rosa massif, between the Nordend and the Dufourspitze, is the highest pass in the Alps – the Silbersattel (4517m).

Why 'Rosa?'

The origin of the name 'Rosa' is lost in the mists of time. One version has it that the name comes from the beautiful pink colour (*rosa*) that tints wide glaciers and snowfields at sunset and sunrise, when the first and last light of day hits the different faces of the massif. When seen from the low valleys and big cities such as Turin and Milan Monte Rosa appears huge and magical, almost floating on a thin layer of clouds. When the sun goes down, the last rays of light bathe the mountains with a strange palette of colour. However, this interpretation could just be romantic nonsense. It seems more likely that the name 'rosa' comes from an ancient dialect word *rouèse* or *roises*, meaning 'glacier'.

First ascents

The achievements of the earliest explorers of the Monte Rosa summits are undocumented… how can we know how many crystal hunters or shepherds tried to climb these peaks? But the first recorded ascent of the Monte Rosa massif is said to have taken place in 1778, when seven Italians from Gressoney went up from the south side, lured by tales of a mythical lost valley. The high point reached by this group (at about 4000m) was called the 'stone of discovery'.

Recent history of mountaineering on the massif is firmly linked to Italian priests: the first ascent belongs to Alagna's priest, Pietro Giordani. He reached 4046m (now called Punta Giordani) in 1801. To Giuseppe Zumstein belongs the ascent of the Zumsteinspitze (4563m) in 1819, and to N Vincent goes the ascent of the Piramide Vincent (4215m) in 1819.

In 1842 another priest, Gnifetti (a name associated with many Monte Rosa peaks), reached the Punta Gnifetti

Ibex at Bettaforca with the Parrotspitze summit behind seen from Stage 3

(Signalkuppe) (4554m). In 1861 an English expedition (EN and TF Buxton and JJ Cowell) climbed Nordend (4612m) with two Guides. In July 1855 an English expedition (J Birkbeck, C Hudson, E Stephenson, and J and C Smyth), with Swiss Guides, attained the highest summit of the range, the Dufourspitze (4634m).

The first difficult route, the Nordend East, was climbed by an Italian expedition (led by Guide L Brioschi) in 1876, and the first winter ascent belongs to another Italian expedition (L Bettineschi, F Jacchini, M Pala and L Pironi) in February 1965.

GLACIERS

Glaciers and glaciated mountains feature strongly all along the Tour of Monte Rosa. The valleys have been carved by the ice, and many people now come to the Alps to see what remains of these huge frozen rivers. The terrain encountered on the trek has been largely shaped by glaciers – mainly long gone – and all around are high snowy mountains. The trek has one short passage on a glacier which, although quite flat and apparently banal, should not be underestimated.

Glaciers respond to climatic changes. In cold periods with heavy snowfall glaciers expand downwards, only to retreat in warm dry periods. Over the course of the centuries the climate has changed more than once, and these fluctuations have influenced the life of the Alpine populations.

The Middle Ages were a time of relative warmth which favoured the colonisation of the Alps at increasingly high altitudes. Glaciers retreated considerably and artefacts found at now-glaciated passes are evidence that much of this terrain was ice-free for many centuries. The 16th century saw the beginning of the Little Ice Age, a cold period of heavy snowfalls which lasted three centuries, and the glaciers regained much territory. The advancing glaciers buried many of the high pastures and gave rise to fear and superstition among mountain people – the ice was literally pushing up against their front doors, and they were moved to call the priests to exorcise these demonic forces.

The mid-19th century saw the start of the warm period which has continued, with occasional colder intervals, to this day. The extent to which we are now in a natural cycle or whether the recent fast melting of the glaciers is due to the effects of modern civilisation may be debated, but there is no doubt that the current warming is very rapid.

ANCIENT PASSES

Many of the trails used by the Tour of Monte Rosa have been used for centuries for all sorts of different purposes. In the Middle Ages the Alpine climate was warmer by several degrees than it is today, and before motorised transport it was often easier and safer to go over the high mountain passes than to descend to the main valleys such as the Rhône and the Aosta. Frequently the mountain valleys were rendered impassable by deep gorges, or were prone to rockfall or landslides. While the high passes carried their own risks – bad weather, cold, exhaustion, attack from marauders – they were usually more direct and less tortuous.

There were abundant reasons for wanting to travel from one valley to the next.

- Trade: in times past people bartered goods rather than dealing in money. Goods that were needed in the Alps included salt and spices, so the mountain people would take their own goods to trade. The wines from the Aosta Valley were sent over to the Valais and Tarentaise by the so-called Route des Vins (which went from Chambave to the Rhône Valley, probably across the Theodul and Collon passes).
- The farmers would take their cattle over into neighbouring valleys to graze as part of the transhumance method of farming.
- People travelled surprisingly long distances for work; for example much of the Alpine architecture in Switzerland is based on the work of Italian builders from the Valsesia region, near Alagna.
- Sometimes people needed to migrate because they had too many enemies in their native valley, or conditions had made survival there untenable.

History tantalises us with fascinating stories about these travels – fortunes lost, treasures found, lives risked. Now as we trek through the mountains, generally comfortable in our high-tech gear and with well-filled stomachs, it's interesting to try to imagine the trepidation that travellers hundreds of years ago would have felt before setting out on these highly risky ventures. The vagaries of Alpine weather meant that any excursion into the hills brought with it a risk of bad weather, not to mention illness or even attack. The frequent presence of chapels and crosses en route attests to the need to put their life in God's hands. Hence on several cols in the Alps – such as the Grand St Bernard, Petit St Bernard and Simplon – we find hospices, erected by religious people to provide safe haven for those poor souls in need of food, shelter or security while trying to get to the next valley.

Theodulpass (3301m)

This pass is one of the most famous in the western Alps and a major crossing point on the Tour of Monte Rosa trek. In Roman times it was called Silvius, and is documented as early as AD3. The name Theodulpass dates from the late 17th century. It was named after St Theodul, a Christian missionary and the first Bishop of Valais towards the end of the fourth century. He made numerous visits to Italy, probably via this pass which now bears his name.

The Monte Moro Pass (L to R): the lift station, the Oberto Maroli hut and the golden Madonna (Stage 6)

In 1895 54 coins dating from 2BC to AD4 were found just below the col, and these are now in an archaeological museum in Zermatt. It must certainly have been hotter and drier in those days, since these and other artefacts attest to the passage of the col on foot and on horseback. It would seem there was a small settlement on the col providing provisions and guided passage. From the 5th century onwards winters became more rigorous and the glaciers began to grow. Commercial caravans abandoned the route, but from the 9th century the glaciers regressed and there was a return of activity across the pass, with several monastic orders settling on both sides of the massif. In 1792 Horace Benedict de Saussure (famed as the main instigator of the first ascent of Mont Blanc) came this way and spent some time at the col measuring the exact altitude of the Matterhorn. Whilst there he apparently found the remains of an old fort built in 1688 by the Comte de Savoie.

The Little Ice Age from the 16th century onwards led to colder conditions and the glaciers grew accordingly. Cols such as the Theodulpass became more and more difficult to cross and would-be travellers were regularly victims of accidents while attempting this passage, be it from the cold, avalanches or crevasses. In 1825 a merchant fell into a crevasse with his horse, allegedly taking 10,000 francs with him – an incentive for bounty hunters for years to come.

In the 20th century conditions on this pass became much easier – in 1910 a herd of 34 cows successfully made the passage – but, nevertheless, care must be taken here.

THE WALSER COMMUNITY

The Italian part of the Tour of Monte Rosa passes through several areas of Walser settlement. The Walsers are descended from Germanic peoples who, a thousand years ago, left their homeland to migrate throughout the Alps. They came from the German-speaking Upper Valais region – in German 'Wallis', hence Walliser people, giving the name 'Walser'. Why they left their homeland is not known – possibly a natural catastrophe, climatic change, plague or a desire to roam – but wherever they settled they preserved their ancient German language, customs and traditions.

They settled in the higher reaches of the Alps, not just in Italy but also in the Swiss Bernese Oberland and the Chablais region of France. They particularly favoured the southern Alpine valleys, especially those surrounding Monte Rosa. The Walser colonisation was achieved peacefully, as the Italian feudal lords in the Valsesia Valley had little to lose in granting them high-altitude land (generally above 1500m or even higher) which was regarded as inhospitable and therefore not exploited by the locals.

In return for maintaining these Alpine lands the Walsers were

Monte Rosa towers over the hamlet of Alpe Bors (Stage 4)

(L to R) Signalkuppe, Zumsteinspitze and Dufourspitze seen from Nordend

allowed freedom. Their communities were not subject to the laws of the region, and in effect they had their own sovereignty. The newcomers did not immediately establish relations with the locals, and initially received supplies of staple commodities such as salt, metal tools, cereals and clothing from the Valais. Later the colonies became practically self-sufficient and the umbilical cord linking them with their old country was broken. Their integration became complete when their self-governing parishes were recognised.

The inhabitants of these isolated colonies had to work hard to survive: they had to clear forest, till the land, create fields and meadows for cultivation and grazing, build houses and, during the summer, produce everything necessary to feed their families and animals during the long winter months. Their ethnic and linguistic isolation and difficulties in communication and transport made them fiercely independent and proudly free. They say that to breathe the air of the Walsers is to breathe the air of freedom.

The Walser culture is expressed not only through language and traditions but can also be seen in their traditional architecture and settlement patterns. The Walsers had to survive in rough conditions, so they became experts in farmwork, making tools and cultivating crops at altitude.

Their houses were often built of wood and these buildings can be seen today (such as at the hamlet of Otro, above Alagna) and will be strung with tools, their large balconies supporting wooden frames for drying hay. Essential to the Walsers' diet was rye bread, baked twice a year (in spring and autumn) in the communal oven. During the winter months it was kept on a special wooden rack hung out from the walls, to prevent attack by mice.

Those houses high in the meadows were isolated from each other to provide larger areas for cultivation around each one. In the towns, such as Alagna and Macugnaga, the houses were clustered together in small groups called *frazioni* (hamlets). Each hamlet, surrounded by a large area of fields, consisted of up to 12 private houses and some communal structures such as the chapel, one or more watermills, a big oven and a stone fountain, which always represented the focal point of the community. This decentralisation of the hamlets was carried out for reasons of safety (to avoid mass destruction through avalanches, landslides and flooding) as well as to gain the maximum amount of sunshine and to make use of local water supplies. In every hamlet the houses were built close together so that the roofs were almost touching, thus protecting the narrow lanes below from rain and snow.

This concentration of dwellings enabled quick and easy access to the

The Otro Valley (Stage 4)

communal services and to the cultivated fields. Walser houses could provide shelter for two or more families, together with their cattle. Stable, dwelling and barn – all the basic needs for the survival of mountain farming people – were concentrated under a single roof. Time for the Walsers was regulated by the seasons, as it still is for many country people, and their society was organised by common rules: everybody had to help build the houses, members of each family had to co-operate in snow shovelling and street maintenance, and so on.

Today the Walser community maintains its unique culture, architecture and language, albeit on a limited scale. Take the time to study the villages and hamlets encountered along the Tour to better understand the harsh way of life endured in these mountain communities. There is a Walser Museum in Alagna (www. alagna.it/en and click on 'Alagna' and then 'The Walser Today') and also one at Macugnaga in the hamlet of Borca.

THE VALLEYS

Monte Rosa and its neighbouring summits form a huge massif from which glaciers descend on both the Swiss and Italian sides, flowing into valleys. On the Swiss side two main valleys, the Mattertal and the Saastal, drain down to the Rhône Valley, while on the Italian side it is a little more complicated. The Valtournanche, the Ayas Valley and the Lys Valley all descend to meet the Aosta Valley, where the main river is the Dora Baltea. The Valsesia drains down to the Po while the River Anza, which flows down the Anzasca Valley from Macugnaga, flows into Lake Maggiore.

Mattertal

Mattertal means 'valley of meadows'. Legend has it that long ago, before the Alps were discovered by climbers and walkers – when mountains were still regarded as the abode of evil spirits and dragons – people believed that a magic valley existed, hidden among the glaciers of Monte Rosa, among the big peaks. It is said that in 1788 a band of men set out from the Valle di Lys in Italy in search of this Eldorado. They climbed over the pass between Monte Rosa and Liskamm (now the Lysjoch) and looked down to the valley below. However, they were disappointed only to find more glaciers, rocks, snowfields and deep ravines. Where were the grassy meadows, the land of milk and honey, which they had been looking for? Perhaps they would not be so disappointed now, seeing how the dawn of mountaineering and the consequent explosion in tourism have made this valley a haven for holidaymakers and a most lucrative place for the inhabitants.

Saastal

The Saas Valley is surrounded by well-known 4000m peaks such as the Dom, Täschhorn, the Allalinhorn, the Strahlhorn, the Rimpfischhorn, the Weissmies, the Lagginhorn… Settlements in the valley go back to the days of the Celts. The inhabitants of the Saas Valley used to form a self-contained community, but in 1392 the area was divided into four politically independent communities. Each settlement retained the basic name 'Saas', the origin of the names Saas Almagell, Saas Balen, Saas Grund and Saas Fee.

For centuries merchants and traders roamed through the Saas Valley across the Monte Moro and Antrona mountain passes to Italy. These trade routes were also used by pilgrims. Even the Romans used to cross these cols, attested by the discovery of ancient coins at the Antrona Pass in 1963. Although the villages in the Saastal grew during the early 20th century, Saas Fee was not developed for tourism until much later, perhaps because access to this higher village was more difficult. The first Saas Fee hotel was constructed in 1880. In 1951 the road up from Saas Grund to Saas Fee was finally completed.

Valtournanche

Dominated by the Matterhorn (or rather Monte Cervino, to give it its Italian name), this Italian valley really represents the Valle d'Aosta. Its first language traditionally was French, hence 'Breuil' in the name of the village at the head of the Mattertal. The valley has its base down at Chatillon, south of Aosta. The Marmore river runs along the valley, draining the glaciers of the Dent Hérens, Matterhorn and Plateau Rosa peaks, among others.

Ayas Valley

This valley is formed by the Evançon river. Its highest village is St Jacques and it meets the main Aosta Valley at Verrés.

Lys Valley

Often known as the Gressoney Valley this is a long and winding gorge that descends from the slopes of Liskamm following the route of the Lys river all the way to Pont St Martin. It is a valley rich in history with several interesting churches and villages.

Valsesia

With its base away down near Novara, far closer to Milan than Aosta, the Valsesia Valley winds its way up to Varallo where the road splits, then continues up to another junction at Balmuccia. The glacier-fed River Sesia gushes down here, and the valley above this point is known as Upper Valsesia. Alagna Valsesia is the highest village in the valley and is surrounded by mountains. This is the home of the Walsers, emigrés from the north via the Valais (Wallis) region (in what is now Switzerland) from the 10th century. Today you'll still hear people speaking the old dialect, based on long-extinct Old German.

Anzasca Valley

This is the most eastern valley coming down from the Monte Rosa massif. It

*Macugnaga seen from
the summit of Nordend*

is very close to the Swiss frontier and it descends from Macugnaga to meet the Toce river near Domodossala, the main access point for Macugnaga, on the main road and railway from Visp/ Brig to Milan. The Toce river flows down into Lake Maggiore, a famous tourist spot.

THE MAIN TOWNS

Saas Fee
Saas Fee lies in an idyllic valley surrounded by the highest mountains in the Swiss Alps. No less than 13 peaks of 4000m or more encircle the village, which has christened itself 'the Pearl of the Alps'.

Saas Fee can be reached by car or bus. No cars are allowed to enter the town (they have to be left in a car park at the entrance to the town); only small electric vehicles operate on the streets (and some petrol-driven refuse trucks). The resort buzzes in both summer and winter, and features the highest underground funicular railway in the world (the Metro-Alpin), which in winter serves the skiing area. It also takes the visitor to the highest revolving restaurant in the world, at 3500m. The campus of the European Graduate School, a university of the Valais canton, is located in Saas Fee.

In old documents Saas is also called Sayxa, Sausa, Solxa and Solze, from the Latin *salix* meaning pasture. The origins of the word 'Fee' have not been established, but it could come from *vee* (cattle), *ves* (mountain), *fö* or *föberg* (sheep mountain) or *fei* (fairy).

Traditional costumes in Saas Fee

Although the region was described by S Grunert in his 18th-century travel book as the 'most abominable wild region of Switzerland', people started to visit the Saas Valley towards the late 18th century and early 19th century precisely because they were attracted by that sort of landscape. They included authors of travel books, cartographers, mineralogists, botanists and landscape painters. Saas Fee was somewhat cut off from the valley until the main road from Saas Grund was constructed in 1951, resulting in an increase in tourism. Despite the influences of modern life, many traditional customs exist to this day, including home-made costumes (which are worn at various events) and traditional music. There are several costume and music societies which can be seen at festivals and parades.

Zermatt

Zermatt is a town of contrasts. Dominated by the Matterhorn, it is nowadays assured a place high on the list for many people travelling in the Alps. With the advent of European travel in the 18th century the inhabitants of Zermatt quickly became aware that they were sitting on a potential goldmine, and since then the town has developed in line with the huge commercial success of the Matterhorn's image. However, it still maintains its mountaineering roots and is a Mecca for alpinists.

Zermatt means 'to the meadows' (*zer* being 'to' and *matt* meaning

27

One way to travel in Zermatt

'meadow'). However, 500 years ago Zermatt was still called Prato Borno, named by the Romans many years before and meaning 'cultivated field'. Zermatt has been a settlement since ancient times – apparently there was a scattering of tiny dwellings there as early as AD100 – but until about AD1100 there was no real central settlement. For centuries it was a place of trade and exchange between neighbouring valleys. Zmutt, situated just above Zermatt – today just a small hamlet with a good view and nice restaurants – was in those days the last place en route to the Theodulpass between Italy and Switzerland, and thus an important spot with its customs post, inns and guiding service for the passage to the col.

As the climate began to change (in the 12th century), the Theodulpass gradually became impassable for parts of the year, and the village that had existed there was abandoned. The 16th–18th centuries were particularly cold – the Little Ice Age – and the glaciers advanced right down to the valleys. The passage of the cols became impracticable, even in summer. Life was almost impossible in the high villages, and many people moved away.

In the early 1800s climatic conditions began to improve, and for the first time foreign tourists visited the Zermatt Valley. As first they were greeted with hostility and mistrust, but gradually the villagers started to set up inns to accommodate these travellers. Until the carriage road was built from

St Niklaus in 1858–60, Zermatt could only be reached on foot or by mule along a rough path. Yet many illustrious visitors, ranging from mountaineers to artists to explorers, were attracted to the unique experience of the town. The arrival of the railway for summer use in 1891 proved a real boost to tourism. The introduction of skiing to the Alps in the early 1900s assured the area's future, but also the relentless exploitation of Zermatt, as it did all other Alpine resorts – the term 'White Gold', used to describe the snow, has proved to be very apt.

It was only in the 1960s that the route as far as Täsch was made into a proper road. Zermatt town council agreed that cars would not be allowed into town, and in 1972 the inhabitants rejected a proposal for a public road to Zermatt. So the town remains car-free, although the silent electric vehicles used throughout town are arguably far more dangerous as they sneak up behind unsuspecting pedestrians. In 1979 the Klein Matterhorn cable car, at 3820m the highest in Europe, was completed.

Breuil-Cervinia

Breuil was the original name of this village, nestled at the top of the valley under the slopes of Monte Cervino and frequented since Roman times. 'Cervinia' was the name given by the fascists under Mussolini during World War II, when they wanted to destroy

On top of the Breithorn, on top of the world!

the long-standing Francophile culture of the Aosta region. The Valdôtain people (of the Aosta Valley) refused this attempted reversal of their culture and took up arms, retreating to the hills and waging a war of resistance. After the liberation most places resumed their French names, but at Breuil-Cervinia they kept both names – presumably the incorporation of the Italian name for the Matterhorn, Cervino, was regarded as a good tourist attraction.

Breuil-Cervinia is a fairly typical resort town with a mix of old and new. The church sports a rather fine sundial and there are some attractive houses, but in general the architecture is not exceptional.

Gressoney St Jean and Gressoney la Trinité

Gressoney St Jean is a located on a wide, lush plain. The surrounding landscape is very interesting because of the excellent view of the majestic mountain ranges and of the Liskamm Glacier, from which the Lys river emerges and runs down the valley.

In the centre of the village some well-preserved Walser houses surround the parish church, dedicated to St John the Baptist. This church was rebuilt in 1725 on the ruins of a previous edifice dating from 1515. Its roof has a big overhang, and the 16th-century bell tower is characterised by a spire and mullion windows. In the parish museum visitors can admire a big crucifix dating back to the middle of the 13th century, probably one of the oldest masterpieces in the Aosta Valley. Not far from the village centre is a charming small lake, whose emerald green water reflects numerous mountain peaks. In 1894 Queen Margherita ordered a castle (Castel Savoia) to be built in this panoramic spot, known nowadays as 'Belvedere', and often holidayed here. One of the best examples of Walser culture is undoubtedly the women's traditional red and black costume with a white blouse trimmed with lace and a precious bonnet made of golden filigree. These can be seen during local festivals, one of which is St John's Feast that begins on the evening of 23 June, when fires are lit in different villages, and lasts for three days. On this occasion the inhabitants of Gressoney go to Mass wearing their traditional costumes.

Gressoney la Trinité has limited facilities – pharmacy, hotels, a shop. Gressoney St Jean has far more, including some quite unexpected shops for such a small town, and there is a regular bus service between the two villages. Between Gressoney la Trinité and Gressoney St Jean there is a marble quarry.

Alagna

Officially named Alagna Valsesia, this charming village (an ancient Walser settlement) is situated in the upper Valsesia at 1205m and is one of the most important ski resorts in Piedmont. Nestling at the foot of Monte Rosa, it is also the starting point for a number

The chapel at Otro (Stage 4) sports a typical fresco

31

of beautiful mountain walks. The village is full of reminders of its Walser origins. In the hamlet of Pedemonte, just a short way from the centre of Alagna, is the Walser Museum, a wonderful record of Walser life. There are also the remains of a 16th-century castle.

The parish church of St John the Baptist in the centre of Alagna is also well worth a visit. The present church was built on the site of an older chapel dating from 1511, and the main altar is an authentic masterpiece of 17th-century baroque work. The village is known for its wood art, and there is evidence of the skilled work of traditional wood artists who were active up and down the Valsesia Valley. There is also a history of mining at Alagna. The main evidence for this is the feldspar mine seen on the road up to Rifugio Pastore, but at one time gold was also mined here.

On the far side of the centre of Alagna lie the hamlets of Dosso, Piane, Rusa and Goreto, typical Walser settlements where little churches provide the centrepoint for a cluster of *baite*, the Walser chalets.

The whole of this area falls under the protection of the Upper Valsesia National Park.

Macugnaga

The small town of Macugnaga feels far from anywhere. If you have to bail out from here it's actually easier to get back to Switzerland than to the Italian valleys further along the trek.

Macugnaga has a colourful past, being not only a high Alpine settlement but also having a history of goldmining. That is long gone now and the town survives mainly on its winter season when people come to ski under the slopes of Monte Rosa. Again the Walser community has made its mark, and there are several fine examples of Walser architecture.

The town is centred round its main square where most of the hotels and bars are situated. As soon as you leave the square you enter quiet old side streets, the silence only broken by the roar of the Anza torrent, swelled by glacial melt during the summer months.

WILDLIFE AND VEGETATION

Plants and flowers

The plants and flowers encountered on any trek vary throughout the year, and even though an Alpine trek of this nature can only be done as a regular walk during the summer months there is a huge change in vegetation between late June and late September. Early on in the summer season the lower slopes around the villages will be a blaze of colour as all the meadow flowers are in bloom up to around 2000m – trumpet gentians, pasque flowers, alpenrose, vetch, martagon lilies...a perfect time to be walking at lower altitudes.

Higher up there may still be nevé remaining from winter, and most slopes will only just be snow-free, so the flowers will not yet be in bloom. As the summer progresses many of the lower meadows will be scythed for haymaking, but above 2000m the flowers will start to bloom. Again the alpenrose – a member of the azalea family – is prevalent, covering the slopes from about 1500 to 2500m. Its pink flowers make a wonderful backdrop for hiking, and trekking in the Alps when these flowers are in season is an absolute joy. Many Alpine flowers that grow at lower altitudes will also be found here, but in a smaller and more intensely coloured form. The houseleeks that grow on the rocks, astrantia and orange hawksbeard are all Alpine versions of regular garden flowers. Above 2500–3000m are the real Alpine gems, tiny jewel-like flowers, so small that they get lost in the rocky crevices. These have a very short growing season of about six weeks before the return of the snows. Hence their miniature, energy-efficient size, and bright colours to maximise their attractiveness to pollinating insects. Look out for starry blue gentians and clumps of pink rock jasmine on the high rocky passes, as well as the rare King of the Alps which you may be lucky enough to spot on a couple of the cols. Scree slopes are often home to the amazing purple and orange toadflax, while

Hardy alpine flowers have to endure extremes of temperatures and very barren ground

on the highest ground you'll find the pinky white buttercup-like flowers of the glacier crowsfoot, allegedly the flower that grows at the highest altitude in the Alps.

The flower everyone expects to see is the edelweiss and you should spot some somewhere along this trek, providing it is not too early in the season – it doesn't generally bloom before mid-July. Although the edelweiss has become known as the classic Alpine flower, many people are disappointed at first sight – its white furry bracts can appear rather grey. Look closely, however, and you'll see that the real flower is the yellow centre, and seen in sunlight it is rather fine.

In September the meadows will no longer be full of flowers, but a keen eye will still spot many different species at higher altitudes. Lower down there will be a few late-season blooms such as purple monkshood growing next to streams, or the Alpine pansy, which seems to keep going for the whole summer. In late summer the lower paths will be bordered by bilberry bushes, laden with berries, and also raspberries, the lure of which makes for slow progress at times. There are also some low-growing bushes bearing shiny red bear berries, used to make a savoury jelly.

There is a wide variety of trees to be found, depending on altitude. The Alps are known for their coniferous forests, largely composed of spruce and pine. These forests are brightened up by larch trees, the only deciduous conifers, which lose their needles each winter. They are a pleasant light green colour in spring, and their needles turn golden before falling in the autumn. Larch is one of the best woods for construction, and most old chalets are made at least in part from this beautiful red wood.

A tree peculiar to the Alps is the Arolla pine (*Pin cembro*) which has long needles and is often seen on the upper limit of the treeline – the higher up it grows, the smaller and more stunted it is. This extremely hardy tree can resist temperatures as low as −50°C and is indifferent to soil quality or slope aspect. Its wood is one of the most sought after, especially by sculptors. Its cones are sturdy, and the seeds too heavy to be blown by the wind. They are eaten by birds, notably the nuthatch, which stores seeds in cracks in rocks. Hence the Arolla pine is classically found growing out from the most improbable boulders.

Wildlife

One of the highlights of walking in the mountains is the excitement of spotting wildlife. In the Alps you may see a whole host of animals and birds along the trail. The chamois, ibex and marmot are the three 'must-sees', but plenty of other animals also inhabit these mountain valleys, meadows and boulderfields. In the forests are several types of deer, generally seen early in the morning or at dusk. Wild boar live below about 1500m and their

Ibex are often seen on the more remote parts of the Tour

snuffling antics often churn up the edges of the footpaths. The chewed pine cones lying on the trail betray the presence of squirrels, which will probably be spotted nipping from tree to tree.

If you are first on the trail you have the best chance of a wildlife sighting, but don't make too much noise or you will scare everything away. The meadows and rocks are home to the mountain hare, which is very timid and more often seen in winter – or at least its tracks are – and the stoat which scampers around rocks, curious but very fast. They say there are lynx in the Alps but they are either very rare or very cautious: seeing one would be quite a surprise.

Wolves are being reintroduced into the Wallis region, but you would be unlikely to catch a glimpse of one.

Above there is a wealth of birds, ranging from the very small to the very big. Any forest walk will be accompanied by the happy chirping of tits, finches and goldcrests, and the drilling of busy woodpeckers. Buzzards are common at the lower levels and, higher up, golden eagles are not rare, especially on bad-weather days when they circle far above on the air currents. On the high cols you will be joined by Alpine choughs the moment you get out your picnic. These black birds, recognisable by their yellow beaks, are known to live at altitudes as high as 8000m in the Himalayas. But the

35

Stoats often play among the rocks

king of all the birds has to be the lammergeier or bearded vulture, reintroduced throughout the Alps over the last few years. You would be lucky to spot one, but if you see a huge bird with an orange underbelly that only seems to flap once an hour it is probably a lammergeier. These giants, long regarded as meat-eating predators, live almost entirely off the bones of dead animals, dropping the bones from on high to break them up for easier consumption. Just rarely you may see a heap of broken bones lying near the trail.

It is a great privilege to see any of these creatures, and while taking photographs is a superb way to immortalise the moment, it is crucial to leave the animal undisturbed. Besides, there's nothing so ridiculous as watching a would-be photographer stalking his subject while the animal moves further

and further away! Fit your camera with a strong zoom lens, or be satisfied to keep the memory in your head.

WHEN TO GO

The Tour of Monte Rosa crosses cols often close to 3000m, which are likely to remain snowy well into June. The huts used on the trek generally do not open until late June or early July, so it is not advisable to set out before the summer Alpine season begins. However, later is not necessarily better as fresh snow is quite likely late in the season.

Névé on certain sections of trail can make passage quite difficult – either because the snow is hard and slippery or because it's a hot, late afternoon and the snow has melted and doesn't hold your weight. For example, the stage from Testa Grigia to Plan Maison/Cime Bianche is really only feasible when there is no snow on the slopes, be it névé or fresh snow. Similarly the climb to Monte Moro from Mattmark can be very tricky in névé or fresh snow as there is a passage across sloping rocky slabs which is aided by cables.

In addition to thinking about snow conditions, you have to decide if you are going to walk every part of the route or whether you intend to take the occasional lift. If you're planning to take lifts, be sure of their open season – usually early to mid-July to early September. In line with the lift season, the hotels in villages such as Macugnaga have a short summer season.

The wild and scenic Ruesso Valley leading up to the Gabiet Lake (Stage 3A)

The best time to do this trek is during this brief summer holiday season – late July to late August. The earlier you go, the more flowers there will be on the hillsides; the middle of the season sees the most holidaymakers in the Alps; the end is generally noted for beautiful autumn light, but can be prone to fresh snowfall above 3000m.

If in doubt call local tourist offices or the huts for up-to-date information on conditions.

GETTING THERE

Zermatt/Saas Fee
By air

The nearest airports are Zurich and Geneva. From Britain these airports are served by many airlines, including British Airways (www.britishairways. com), Easyjet (www.easyjet.com), Swiss International (www.swiss.com). Aer Lingus (www.aerlingus.com) fly to Geneva from Ireland.

Onward travel to Zermatt or Saas Fee is best done by train.

By train

Eurostar run a regular service from London to Geneva, which takes about 6 hours (www.eurostar.com) and for travelling around once in Switzerland the train service does not disappoint. The Swiss railway network is incredibly efficient; timetables and online ticket sales can be found at www.sbb. ch. For the best prices it may be worth buying a Swiss rail pass – all the different passes are described in detail on www.myswissalps.com/swissrailpasses with helplines and forums to advise on the best choice of pass.

By car

If you drive to Switzerland you'll need to buy a motorway *vignette* on entry to the country, which in 2014 cost 40CHF for the year – this price has been held for years and each year there is talk of a considerable hike in price, so don't be surprised if it costs more than this in the future. You cannot take the car to Zermatt, but must park at Täsch and take the train up to the town. Saas Fee is also a car-free resort with a large paying car park at the entrance to the town. The other Saas villages, notably Saas Grund, all allow cars and have lots of parking areas.

By bus

Eurolines offer a regular service from Britain and Ireland to Switzerland, serving both Geneva and Zurich. Although the journey is long the price is competitive: www.eurolines.com tel: 08717 818178.

Breuil-Cervinia/Gressonney/Alagna
By air

The nearest airport is Turin (www. aeroportoditorino.it). The other option is Milan Malpensa (www.milanom alpensa-airport.com). Turin and Milan Malpensa airports are served by various airlines, including British Airways (www.britishairways.com) and Easyjet (www.easyjet.com).

By train

There is a train service from Milan to Turin and a train and bus service from Turin to Aosta, then good bus services up the valley to Breuil-Cervinia. There is no direct connection from Turin or Milan to Cervinia; you have to change buses at Châtillon. The bus stations are in the city and not at the airports.

By car

Driving in Italy is generally good fun so long as you have an adventurous spirit. The motorways usually charge tolls.

By bus

Eurolines offer a regular service from Britain and Ireland to Italy with stops at Turin and Aosta and Châtillon (at the bottom of the valley up to Cervinia): www.eurolines.com tel: 08717 818178.

Access to other towns

From Zurich, Geneva or Turin airports you can reach any of the other towns encountered during the trek. In Switzerland the train is the best way to get along the main valleys, from where the yellow Swiss PTT buses give access to all but the remotest villages. These tend to meet up with the trains, so travel is exceptionally easy. There is also train access along the Aosta Valley from Turin and Milan, with buses up the side valleys.

GETTING AROUND

There are several possibilities for using lifts during the Tour of Monte Rosa. These can be very useful for a number of reasons. If you are pressed for time,

The marvellous trail leading down from Colle del Turlo on Stage 5

using a lift could cut off several hours of walking, and if your knees are hurting, taking a lift down could make all the difference to your comfort on the rest of the trip. Furthermore, lifts are inevitably in ski areas, and some of these look a lot better when covered in snow. So to avoid walking up or down bulldozed pistes it may be a good idea to take the lift – the ascent from Stafal (Gressoney) to the Passo dei Salati springs to mind, as does the descent from Testa Grigia to Plan Maison.

However, it is important to bear in mind that the lifts have a very limited open season in the summer. Typically this may be from the first week or even the second week of

July to the first week of September, so if these are an integral part of your trek planning you need to be absolutely sure they will be running. If they are just an option this is less crucial, though once you've decided to take a lift, finding it closed can be a very traumatic experience! It's worth knowing that some lifts have a timetable in the summer (rather than running continuously) and they tend to close for lunch or close early afternoon to fit in with summer skiing requirements.

Buses are a useful means of escape if you have to abandon the trek for some reason, or if you only plan to do a part of it. Most of the bus services mentioned in this guide are year-round regular services, but the frequency can change radically outside the high summer season. Tourist offices will have details.

ACCOMMODATION

There are a host of accommodation possibilities for your stay, ranging from hotels of all standards to an *auberge* or *albergo* (a basic hotel usually offering dormitory accommodation and maybe small rooms) to huts to campsites. In the summer season – July and August – there is a huge demand for accommodation, so advance booking is highly recommended (see Appendix C for hut contact information and Appendix D for other contacts).

Hotels

These range from 4-star luxury to no-star basic. Major towns such as Zermatt, Breuil-Cervinia and Saas Fee have many to choose from, whereas the smaller villages like St Jacques and Grächen have just a handful, usually in the 2-star category or below. In addition to rooms, some hotels also have a dormitory; this is particularly common in Switzerland. The local tourist offices will provide a list of hotels and may even make bookings for you. Note that some hotels in the Italian towns do not open before early July – this can be the case where there is a cable car (the opening time of the cable car dictates the season for the hotels).

Campsites

There are sites in most Alpine towns. Camping is generally not allowed in the valley outside campsites or (sometimes) near to the huts. Ask the tourist office for details.

Huts or refuges

Mountain huts vary greatly in the facilities they offer, from quite luxurious with showers and even small bedrooms to the most basic with just a dormitory and a dining room. There are always toilets, and running cold water is almost guaranteed, although exceptionally hot summers can lead to isolated cases of dried-up supplies. Huts high in the mountains may not have running water early in the morning when the source could be frozen, so at such huts it's wise to fill water bottles the previous evening. Most huts are open from late June/early July to early September, and there will be a guardian in residence. Usually the guardian cooks an evening meal and provides breakfast. At a few huts you can take your own food, but you must make sure the guardian is happy with this. Quite frankly it is hardly worth the effort of carrying up food when a very good meal will be on offer for a reasonable price. Drinks – alcoholic and otherwise – are also sold.

In Italy there are strict laws about public water supplies and in some huts you may be told that the tap water is not controlled – this means they cannot guarantee that it is clean. If in doubt it's always better to buy water than to risk being ill and unable to hike the next day.

Hut etiquette

Trekkers in the Alps are privileged to have a system of huts that makes it possible to walk with small packs, and to know that at the end of each day there'll be somewhere to sleep and a good hot meal. It's really important to treat the huts and their guardians with the respect they deserve. Book accommodation in advance, even if you just phone the night before; and if you are not going to show up then do call to cancel.

When you arrive at a hut make yourself known to the guardian, who will show you what to do. Each hut has its own system; some are very relaxed and others less so. The guardian will tell you where to leave your rucksack; sometimes you can take it to your room, sometimes not. He will ask you to take off your boots and show you where to put them, as well as where to leave crampons and trekking poles. You are expected to vacate your room by a certain time in the morning and to leave it as you found it; this generally means folding up blankets or quilts. If you have dietary requirements you should tell the guardian when you make your booking so he can prepare a suitable meal. Most huts do not have a huge variety of food available, so unless you really are a vegetarian or really do have a food allergy then it's best to eat whatever you are given. Huts do sell drinks, and sometimes you can run up a tab and pay for everything at

Monte Rosa from Alpenzu (Stage 3A)

the end of your stay. Many huts prefer that you settle the bill before going to bed. Remember that credit cards are not usually accepted, so take cash – euros in Italy; Swiss francs (CHF) in Switzerland. Although sometimes the guardian and friends may party until the small hours it's generally accepted that from 10pm everyone is in bed.

On a trek such as this it is important to get your provisions for the next day's stage the previous day; on some stages there is no guarantee that you will be able to buy food during the day. Many of the huts will make up a picnic if you ask the evening before. If in doubt about the availability of fresh water on the route be sure to take plenty from the hut when you leave.

Most huts do not have road access so everything has to be transported in by helicopter or on foot. Bear this in mind and take your own rubbish down.

REGIONAL HIGHLIGHTS

Zermatt

- It is very highly recommended that you walk the Höhbalmen to experience some of the best scenery possible, especially the views of the Matterhorn. The route goes from Zermatt past Zmutt to the junction with the path to the Schönbielhütte, which is also worth a visit. The Höhbalmen goes right where this path goes

The Stellisee above Zermatt is one of many splendid viewpoints

left, and up onto a high shelf from where there are marvellous views of the Matterhorn, the Mischabel range and the Monte Rosa peaks. On the descent be sure to stop at the Hotel du Trift (Berggasthaus Trift) for some home-made iced tea. If you have time spend the night here in the company of owners Hugo and Fabienne – you will not find a warmer and more informed host than Hugo, who is also a UIAGM/IFMGA Guide.

- Many people like to walk up to the Hörnlihütte to see the start of the ascent of the Matterhorn; if you walk just a little way beyond the hut you can touch the rock of the peak.
- The Gornergrat railway makes for an easy way to view the summits. This train goes up to 3000m altitude and is a very pleasant journey for a rest day. From here the views of the Gorner Glacier and surrounding peaks – including the Monte Rosa peaks – are breathtaking.
- Skiers might be tempted by a day's skiing from the Klein Matterhorn lift, which serves the summer skiing area.
- Switzerland is the land of cheese and chocolate and these are clearly the foods to go for. The local huts and restaurants do a fine line in cheese dishes, as well as *rösti* (grated fried potato).
- Zermatt Museum is a good place to pass a few hours, immersing yourself in the history of the town and the first ascents of the peaks. The rope used by Edward Whymper and friends on the first ascent of the Matterhorn is on display, its frayed broken end a poignant reminder of how quickly victory can turn to disaster in the mountains.

Saas Valley

- At Saas Balen, the first village encountered in the Saas Valley, you can see an enormous variety of Alpine flowers at Heimischgartu (2100m) and by the milky Grüebe Lake. Well worth seeing is the round late-baroque church, a building of national importance, and the roaring Fellbach stream which runs through the middle of the village.
- At the heart of the Saas Valley, Saas Grund offers a wide variety of activities for tourists. From the top of the lifts at Hohsaas (3100m) there is a breathtaking view of all the 18 peaks of 4000m+ which surround the area.
- Saas Almagell is the most southerly village in the Saas Valley. It is a friendly, family-oriented place, which has retained the character of a typical Valais mountain village. The dammed lake at Mattmark is a top tourist attraction.
- Situated 120m above the valley, Saas Fee is a summer and winter resort as well as a thriving small town. The village continues to

exhibit many traditional customs which are deeply rooted in the history of the Saas Valley.

Valtournanche, Val d'Ayas, Lys Valley

- There are bus services down each valley to the main Aosta Valley. Those interested in wine could spend a day checking out some of the vineyards where winetasting is on offer.
- There is a host of castles to visit in the Aosta Valley. Aosta has many well-documented Roman monuments which can be visited on foot.
- The Aosta region has many specialities, notably woodcarvings which are very beautiful to look at, though perhaps a little too heavy to stow away in a rucksack for the rest of the trek.
- Valtournanche is a very attractive village with a particularly fine square by the church. The Bar des Guides has an interesting array of plaques honouring local Guides, past and present.
- If you have transport, the St Barthélemy Valley makes a delightful drive, and you could include a visit to the Astronomy Centre at Lignan.
- The caverns of the Gouffre des Busserailles on the road to Cervinia, 3km after Valtournanche, are worth a visit. Before entering the gorge you can see the *marmitte dei giganti*, water-eroded rocks so-called because of their imposing cauldron shape. A bit further on is the ravine, a fissure in the rock dating from the Ice Age, shaped by the power of the water and glaciers of the Matterhorn which once submerged the valley. Further up there is a 35m-high waterfall.

- St Vincent, down in the main valley, is famous for its thermal baths, open from May to October. There are also Roman ruins under the church of Saint-Vincent and along what remains of the imperial road to Gaul. The present parish church, one of the most ancient in the Aosta Valley, was built on an area of late Gallic buildings and Roman baths. In the parish museum there are woodcarvings, frescos and fresco cartoons.
- The Aosta region is famed for its food, notably Fontina cheese and cold meats. There are many speciality stores that stock a whole range of varieties. Apples are also a traditional Valdôtain product and can be found dried, in juice and in local dishes.

Valsesia

Any spare time would be well spent visiting one of the Walser settlements. Several of these can be easily accessed from Alagna, and the tourist office has lots of information. There is also a paleontology museum down the valley at Borgosesia, with displays of artefacts excavated from prehistoric settlements in caves in the valley.

Since much of the upper valley is a National Park there are plenty of day walks to be done in fabulous scenery.

In the hamlets – apart from the craftsmen's shops – there are also many typical restaurants where you can try *miacce* (a sort of pancake cooked in a special iron pan of Walser origin). Polenta and game are just two of the typical local dishes that can be sampled in the restaurants both in the centre of Alagna and in the hamlets.

Macugnaga

Some really interesting museums give a valuable insight into earlier times at Macugnaga.

- Museo della Montagna at Staffa is located in an old house. On the ground floor are tools of the trade from local Guides as well as details of local first ascents and tragedies. The second floor is devoted to the Walser civilisation in Macugnaga and the Alpine history of Monte Rosa.
- Museo Casa Walser at Borca is an example of typical Walser architecture, the museum being located in an old Walser house.
- Antica Miniera Aurifera della Guia is an ancient goldmine. This is situated near the Walser Museum in Borca. Legend has it that the Romans and Celts found gold in the Anzasca Valley, in impurities in the mineral ores of pyrite and quartzite. Production peaked in the 20th century.

Languages

The Monte Rosa massif lies on the Swiss-Italian border. While in the main centres of Breuil-Cervinia and Saas Fee – and especially Zermatt – English is widely understood, it is worth making an effort to speak the local languages. The shopkeepers and hoteliers have realised that it serves them well to speak English, and many do so to some extent. Notwithstanding this, it is worth trying to learn a few basic words; there is a lot of pleasure to be gained by having a go at communicating in the local language. Most people will meet you halfway and will respect your endeavours in the realm of international relations!

The Swiss part of the walk passes through German-speaking Switzerland. The language is Swiss German, not the High German you might have learned at school, but Swiss people in this region do understand High German. In the Aosta Valley French has, for a long time, been an equal first language (with Italian), and this is often a better alternative to English if you don't speak Italian.

Some useful words are noted in Appendix E, and those relating to the weather can be especially handy if you can't find a forecast in English.

Currencies

With the introduction of the euro it has become very easy to travel around

Dizzy views down to the Saastal from the Höhenweg (Stage 7)

Europe. In Switzerland, however, the Swiss franc (CHF) remains the currency, but some cafés and super-markets will accept euros if that's all you have. The same applies to Swiss mountain huts, but don't expect to get a good rate of exchange. Change will generally be given in francs. In Italy most places won't accept anything except euros.

In the big towns credit cards are generally accepted, and most Alpine towns have at least one ATM. However, remember that up in the hills the only currency is cash, so be sure to take enough.

EMERGENCIES, RESCUE AND INSURANCE

Trekking should not be a high-risk activity, but there are increasing numbers of accidents, even on non-glaciated terrain. This is partly because more and more people walk in the Alps, but it is also a factor of the adventurous terrain that is being accessed by footpaths. Glaciated terrain brings its own objective hazards, but these are minimal on the gentle glacier encountered on the Tour of Monte Rosa. Nevertheless, for all Alpine walking you need to consider emergencies that could arise. If you are well equipped and prepared you will hopefully avoid, or at least know how to deal with, most situations.

First aid

All walkers should carry a basic first aid kit in their rucksacks. Although the trek described here is multi-day, there are opportunities to get medical supplies if needed or to abandon the route for a few days. In addition there are good and reliable rescue services in the Swiss and Italian regions covered, so the first aid kit can be kept to the essentials:

- plasters
- painkillers
- aspirin
- treatment for diarrhoea
- antiseptic cream
- crêpe bandage
- fly repellent
- antihistamine cream
- scissors
- tweezers
- antiseptic wipes
- wound dressing
- blister kit
- latex gloves
- triangular bandage (or use a scarf or bandana)
- bivvy bag or space blanket (shiny foil)

With this kit you should be able to deal with most emergencies that could be encountered during the walk. Resourcefulness is most useful: a trekking pole can be used to splint an injured arm or leg. However, if a problem becomes serious then you should be prepared to leave the trek. It is not recommended to continue if, for example, you have an upset stomach which prevents you eating properly or risks leading to dehydration, or some form of infection, such as a blister that has become ulcerated. Continuing to hike day after day with an ongoing condition could cause long-term damage.

Potential problems on the hill

As well as carrying the gear it's also crucial to know what to do in the event of incidents that can happen during mountain walks:

Heart attack Everyone should have basic first aid knowledge. Treatment of a heart attack victim goes beyond the scope of this guide but should be learnt at a first aid centre. This is knowledge that is hopefully never used, hence the need for regular refresher courses.

Hypothermia If you are walking in the summer months you would not expect to be at risk of hypothermia, which is generally associated with winter expeditions and high-altitude mountaineering. However, there are a surprising number of incidences of hypothermia each summer in the non-glaciated Alps. On the Tour of Monte Rosa you are flirting with the high mountains and attaining altitudes of nearly 3500m. In classic summer hypothermia cases the victim becomes very hot and consequently sweaty while walking uphill, then cools very quickly, exacerbated by wind chill and tiredness. The same situation can arise during bad weather, when snow is frequent above 2000m even in the summer.

The best action to take against hypothermia is to avoid it in the first place. When the summit is reached or the wind gets up, put on an extra layer straight away; be sure to eat and drink regularly and don't hesitate to change your planned route if necessary.

Walkers coming up from the Gran Lago on Stage 2

Altitude sickness It is unlikely that true altitude sickness will be encountered on the Tour of Monte Rosa as mostly the trail remains around and below 3000m. Although people may sometimes think they are feeling the effects of high altitude, altitude sickness is really only encountered above 3000m. However, those coming from sea level will certainly feel breathless the first day or so hiking in the Alps. To what extent this is due to the thinner air and to what extent to the inclines is a moot issue. Were you to start immediately with an ascent of the Breithorn it is very likely that you would feel bad, and serious sickness a possibility. When going high be sure to drink plenty of water and, if necessary, take small doses of aspirin for headaches. Stick to lower altitudes for the first few days of a holiday.

Falls The results of falls can range from minor scrapes and grazes to sprained and broken limbs, or worse. The former are obviously easily treated with dressings and antiseptic creams. Sprains can be strapped up effectively, and then the victim can usually make his way down with help. Broken limbs can be splinted using a trekking pole, but whether the victim can walk down depends on where the break is and the severity of it: if in doubt call the rescue service. Anything worse requires help from professionals; back and head injuries are potentially very serious so the victim should not be moved (unless further injury is likely by staying where they are) and the rescue service should be called immediately.

Rescue
Note Rescue and medical costs are charged in Europe, so be sure to have insurance for this before you set off.

Should the unthinkable happen and you do have to call the rescue services, it's reassuring to know that compared to many mountain areas the Alps are relatively friendly in an accident situation. Given good weather you can expect the mountain rescue to arrive within a short time of your call. In Switzerland and Italy there are professional rescue services, using trained rescue personnel, doctors and Guides. They generally operate with helicopters from a base very near town. In bad weather when the helicopter can't fly a rescue party might be sent on foot; this could take a lot longer.

However, calling the rescue should be seen as a last resort. Since mobile phones have become part of the walker's kit list the rescue services get called out for the most trivial of reasons, ranging from tiredness to being late for a restaurant reservation. It should be remembered that having the back up of such a service is a privilege not to be abused.

In the case of a genuine need for rescue this is the procedure:
• Call the rescue services:
  • Italy Aosta Valley 118
  • Switzerland Valais 144 or
  • call 112, which works throughout Europe.

- Have the following information ready:
  - Your name
  - The nature of the accident
  - The number of victims
  - The seriousness of the victim's injuries – is he conscious?
  - Your position, itinerary, altitude
  - The time of the accident
  - The current weather conditions – wind and visibility
- Prepare for the arrival of the helicopter team by putting the injured person in an accessible place. This will not always be possible but, if feasible, find a flat place where the helicopter can land. Do not move an unconscious patient or one who may have back injuries. In all events secure the victim and also all equipment. Keep everyone else away from this area; the helicopter will generate a lot of wind when it arrives.
- Make your position visible, using brightly coloured items such as bivvy bags or rucksacks.
- When the helicopter appears use your arms in the air to make a Y symbol to indicate that you are the people who called for rescue.

Once the team have arrived they will take over. The rescue services in the Alps speak English, so this is probably not the time to try out those new German/French/Italian phrases unless you are reasonably proficient.

It is recommended that walkers in the Alps carry a mobile phone, but only to be used to call the rescue when it is truly necessary. There is telephone network cover in many parts of the Alps, but not everywhere, including on some parts of the Tour of Monte Rosa.

Insurance

Rescue is not free in Switzerland and Italy, nor are hospital and medical costs. An accident could prove very costly, so you need to be insured for rescue from the hill, for medical costs and repatriation. You can get this before leaving home (in the UK try the British Mountaineering Council, or Snowcard). Internationally the Austrian Alpine Club insurance has a good reputation. Make sure the insurance company knows you will be trekking on terrain that is both glaciated and non-glaciated, and that for the former you may use a rope. You will not be climbing. If you cannot get appropriate cover at home then you can get insurance for the period of the trek from Air Zermatt (tel: +41 27 966 86 86; zermatt@air-zermatt.ch).

ALPINE WEATHER

The mountains are affected by general European weather systems, but they also create their own localised anomalies. As a frontal system approaches the Alps the air, laden with moisture from the sea, has to rise over the mountains, resulting in a cooling

Sunrise on the East Face of the Matterhorn seen from the Theodule Glacier on Stage 1

of the air, turning water vapour into droplets and consequently precipitation. The precipitation sometimes falls mainly on one side of the Alps, leaving the other in a rain shadow, enjoying relatively dry conditions. This classically happens in the Monte Rosa massif when, for example, the weather can come from the south, giving heavy rain or snow on the Italian side of the range while the Zermatt Valley is protected and basks in the sun. The opposite is sometimes true when the weather comes from the north. This effect is caused by a *föhn* wind – a southern föhn causes rain on the Italian side of the Alps, a northern föhn means that Italy will be largely dry, while France and parts of Switzerland get the bad weather.

A front can be accompanied by winds from a different direction, for example a westerly front is often accompanied by a southerly föhn, and frequently the wind changes direction after a front has passed.

The Monte Rosa massif forms the first major obstacle to air coming up from the lowlands and lakes and as such can be shrouded in cloud as the warm air rises very quickly and forms water vapour.

Mountain weather can change very suddenly, so always get a weather forecast before heading out. These are available at local tourist offices, Guides' bureaux, and by phone or internet. Appendix D contains some useful sources of information. However, don't stick rigidly by

A shower on the trail to Mattmark after heavy rain (Stage 6)

what is predicted; sometimes fronts come in more quickly or more slowly than anticipated (maybe by up to six hours), an anticyclone can hold off a front for longer than expected, or a very localised change can affect the outcome. Look at the sky and if you see the weather worsening rethink your plans for that day. Classic signs include:

- thin wispy clouds caused by high winds at altitude
- increasing wind in the valleys
- cumulus clouds building in the mountains
- locals carrying umbrellas.

Forecasts are generally put out in the local language – a brief glossary of useful terms is given in Appendix E – but you can always ask at the local tourist offices, where usually somebody has at least a rudimentary knowledge of English.

CLOTHING AND EQUIPMENT

For the Tour of Monte Rosa you need to be equipped for regular summer Alpine trekking, but with some additional gear for glacier crossings (see Glacier travel). This can add a significant amount of weight to your sac, and it may seem a bit over the top for the short Theodule Glacier. However, if you plan to include an ascent of the Breithorn this gear is more worthwhile. If you feel this extra weight is too much for the duration of the trek then consider taking a Guide for the one short glaciated section (see Hiring a guide); the Guide will bring the rope and glacier-travel gear, and the most you will need is a pair of lightweight crampons. You could use the Guide for the Breithorn climb too.

The weather can range from very hot to very cold with all the variations in between. Normal temperatures at 2000m are about 10–15°C in the day; 0°C is usually between 3000m and 3500m. However, during bad weather or storms the temperature can plummet and snow can fall as low as 1500m at any time during the summer. Wind will make the conditions feel even colder, so you need to be prepared for all eventualities. Layers are better than padded or thick garments, and clothes next to the skin should be moisture-wicking and quick-drying – leave the cotton T-shirts at home.

Life in the hills should be seen as a different experience to your normal home life so embrace the simplicity of it and accept that you may well be wearing the same clothes for days

Instep crampons (or high quality microspikes such as Grivels) provide a lightweight solution to the problem of what gear is needed for this trek

at a time. In this way you can keep your sac weight acceptable – nothing spoils a good walk more than having unwanted kilos piled on your back.

Waterproofs are essential, and a waterproof cover for your sac is a good idea, supplemented with a drysac or plastic liner inside your sac. Ankle-high gaiters are the coolest for summer, and will only be needed on the glacier to keep the snow out of your boots. Gloves and fleece hat will complete the cold-weather ensemble.

The rucksack does not need to be huge, especially if you're planning on using huts. However, it does need to be comfortable, and for trekking it's best to have a sac with a padded hip-belt.

Boots can be lightweight so long as they take crampons. The sole is hugely important – it's amazing how a worn sole affects your grip on all sorts of terrain.

Assuming the weather will be mainly sunny you need to go prepared. At altitude those UV rays are that much stronger as you're higher up and there is less pollution to protect you. A sunhat, sunglasses and sun-cream are definitely called for.

Sheet sleeping bags are highly recommended for huts (and are a requirement in Italian huts). Other equipment should include:

• first aid kit
• trekking poles
• water bottle
• food

53

- camera
- compass
- map
- glacier gear.

Glacier travel involves being roped up and having the necessary gear to get yourself or someone else out of a crevasse. Crampons are generally needed to walk on glaciers, but for the short glacier on this trek it is not necessary to have an ice axe – trekking poles will suffice. Conditions on the glacier can vary from soft fresh snow to ice to melted slush. You need to make an informed decision about whether to take crampons for this section, depending on:

- whether you do the trek early or late in the summer season
- whether there was snowfall late in the winter season
- whether it has snowed much recently
- your experience and confidence on glaciers and snow
- local advice before you set off.

If you do not plan to ascend any peaks a pair of instep crampons (or high quality microspikes) will certainly be adequate for the Tour. These are considerably smaller than normal crampons and can be attached to all footwear.

When travelling out by plane for an Alpine trek it is strongly recommended that you wear your hiking boots and put essentials in your cabin bag – raingear, maps, compass...just

The Quarazza Valley and the Colle del Turlo, visible at the far end on the left (Stage 5)

in case your hold bags don't arrive. On trains keep an eye on your bags... it's not a great start to your trek if you find yourself without your gear.

Buying kit out there
Generally you will have all the necessary gear when you arrive in the Alps, but you may need to buy maps, guidebooks, or extra equipment before or during the trek. Zermatt has a vast range of sports shops stocking everything you might (or might not) ever need for the mountains. Maps can be bought from the Wega bookshop (on the High Street opposite the turn-off to the post office). Elsewhere en route there are gear shops in Breuil-Cervinia and Saas Fee, as well as more limited fare in Alagna, Gressoney St Jean and Macugnaga.

MAPS

There are various 1:50,000 maps that each cover the entire Tour of Monte Rosa. The easiest to buy online are:
• Swiss Topo 5028T Monte Rosa Matterhorn
• Tour du Mont Rose L'Escursionista Editore EAN/ISBN: 9788890833410
Otherwise two maps cover the whole route:
• 1:50,000 Istituto Geografico Centrale (IGC) 5 Cervino-Matterhorn e Monte Rosa
• 1:50,000 Carte Nationale de la Suisse 5006 Matterhorn Mischabel

The following 1:25,000 maps cover the Tour:
• 1:25,000 Carte Nationale de la Suisse 1348 Zermatt; 1329 Saas; 1349 Monte Moro; 1328 Randa; 1308 St Niklaus
• 1:25,000 IGC 108 Cervino Matterhorn Breuil Cervinia Champoluc; 109 Monte Rosa Alagna Macugnaga Gressoney
Maps are available locally or from The Map Shop (www.themapshop.co.uk), Stanfords (www.stanfords.co.uk) and Cordee (www.cordee.co.uk).

GLACIER TRAVEL

Glaciers introduce a whole new dimension to walking, notably that of the dangers of crevasses and the need to use crampons and possibly an ice axe. With the right equipment and, far more importantly, the right knowledge, these dangers can be reduced to an acceptable level. This knowledge can be gained in part by reading textbooks, but really there is no substitute for the real thing, either going with experienced friends or by paying for professional instruction by qualified Guides. It is essential that you are trained in glacier travel before venturing onto glaciers during this trek. This section is included because although the glaciated section is very short, it is, nevertheless, a glacier, and some people who trek around Monte Rosa will want to finish by climbing up the Breithorn peak, which is also a

Practising good glacier travel technique on the slopes above the Theodule Glacier

glacier. There is more information on glacier travel in Appendix F.

Glacier-travel guidelines

There are two types of glacier conditions:

- Dry glacier – when the glacier has no fresh snow cover and is purely ice; all crevasses can be seen
- Wet glacier – when fresh snow lies on the ice and hides some or all of the crevasses.

The dry glacier often requires crampons for safe walking but usually, unless it is steep, no rope is required as the crevasses are visible and thus can be avoided. A wet glacier presents more objective dangers as the crevasses are hidden and snow bridges are usually used to cross them

– these can be fragile and collapse at any moment. When you step onto a wet glacier the rule is 'rope up and cover up' – that is, attach the rope and put on long-sleeved shirts and trousers as a fall into a crevasse could be a very cold experience. A glacier may be dry in its lower part but become wet higher up, so always take the rope in case – if in doubt, use it.

Be aware of how the crevasses have formed on the glacier, and when roped up ensure that you are not all at risk at the same time. Crevasses most commonly occur on the edge of convexities, on the outside and inside of bends, at the confluence of two glaciers and around jutting features such as rocky buttresses that project into the glacier. Usually you can plan your route on the glacier from looking carefully at the map and trying to avoid these areas, although this doesn't mean you won't find crevasses on flat parts of glaciers. The rope should be kept reasonably taut at all times, and especially when crossing obviously crevassed areas and delicate snow bridges.

Some glaciers are threatened from higher up by seracs. If you have to walk under a serac wall go as quickly as possible – this is not a good place to stop for a picnic.

Glaciers are best travelled in the morning, when the snow is firm underfoot and the snow bridges over the crevasses are at their most solid. An Alpine dawn is one of the joys of the high mountains, and huts are not the place to have a lie-in since everyone gets up early. If this means you arrive early afternoon at the next hut then enjoy the views and take a nap.

Glacier-travel gear list

- **Crampons**
- **Ice axe** 55–60cm for a normal-size person
- **Harness**
- **Crevasse rescue equipment** 2 prussik loops, a long sling, 5 karabiners (1 screwgate, 1 pear-shaped screwgate [HMS] which can be used for an Italian hitch, 3 snaplinks) and an ice screw. This is a minimum requirement, and you may choose to take other things too.
- **Rope** Dynamic rope of at least 8mm, minimum 30m long. Clearly if there are lots of people in the group more than one rope should be taken, but bear in mind that weight is also an issue. It was thought until recently that a rope should not be used singly if it isn't designed as a single rope, but on

En route to the Breithorn, a straightforward optional peak at the end of Stage 1

glaciers the force generated by falls is not the same as that generated on rock climbs. It is now agreed that 8mm is adequate, provided it is dynamic. However, the downside of a thin rope is that it is harder to grip for rescue manoeuvres, both by hand and with prussiks.

Hiring a guide

For the glacier crossing and/or ascent of the Breithorn you need either to have some experience in glacier travel or to hire a Guide. Both Zermatt and Breuil-Cervinia have Guides' bureaux (see Appendix D). It is best to reserve a Guide a few days in advance and you need to specify what you will be doing. The Guide will generally take up to six people. He will provide the rope and may also bring harnesses and crampons. Certainly this is the case for the Breithorn. For this summit you can hire a Guide from either of the huts on the Plateau Rosa. Again, it is best to do so in advance.

PLANNING YOUR TREK

Which way round?

Being a circular tour, this trek can be started anywhere along the way and can be done in either direction. It is described in this guide in an anti-clockwise direction, starting in Zermatt. This is certainly not the only way to do this trek, and not even the

most common way. The reasons for describing the trek in this manner are summed up below.

Starting in Zermatt means that the first day gets you close to Monte Rosa and you can see parts of the massif and the other high peaks surrounding it. You are therefore immediately acquainted with the glacial world that dictates your route. The downside of this plan is that your first day takes you to the highest altitude encountered on the Tour. Many people start the Tour of Monte Rosa in Saas Fee, which gives them time to get used to the altitude over the first three days to Zermatt. To my mind, however, this option means that you spend a long time trekking around a mountain that you haven't yet seen; and what is more, the long balcony trails of the Höhenweg and the Europaweg are far more strenuous than they might appear on the maps and really do take their toll physically.

One answer to this is to go clockwise from Saas Fee, straight up to Monte Moro Pass and, given good weather, you'll be on intimate terms with Monte Rosa from the start. I have done the Tour many times like this.

So why describe it *anti-clockwise*? One valid reason is that at Macugnaga it can be difficult to get a one-night reservation in a hotel in high season. Going anti-clockwise, if you find that you are unable to get a booking in Macugnaga you can plan to arrive there from the Colle del Turlo at the end of the afternoon and then take the cable car to Monte Moro Pass and stay at the excellent Rifugio Oberto Maroli. Coming clockwise from Saas Fee, if you stay at this hut then the next day would be a very long one to Rifugio Pastore or Alagna, if you walked all the way, but to use the lift you have to wait until about 9am for the first car down to Macugnaga.

Other arguments for this anti-clockwise direction are that the section from the Theodulpass to the Colle Sup. delle Cime Bianche is easier done in descent than ascent (although in snowy conditions it's far wiser to take the cable car), the stage from Gabiet to Pastore is easier clockwise than anticlockwise and the ascent to the Colle Turlo is shorter going up from Pastore than from Macugnaga.

Some people argue that the paths are nicest walked in this anti-clockwise direction, that it gives more options for variations...who knows? There is no right way to do this trek, so look closely at the map and make your own decision. You can be sure that all the other trekkers on the trail will have their own ideas: this is really not a trek where everyone is going the same way and staying at the same huts.

Difficulty of the trek

The Tour of Monte Rosa covers a great variety of terrain, ranging from major forest tracks to narrow single-track footpaths to scree slopes to glacier. You need to be fit, with good balance

Monte Rosa seen from Rifugio Pastore at the end of Stage 4

and the ability to walk on very rough ground. Conditions vary according to the time of year. Early in the summer the snow may only just have melted, and north-facing sections could be icy, slushy or very wet. There may well be obstacles on the paths, such as trees that have fallen down during the winter. As the summer goes on the trail generally becomes more worn and clear of debris. Signposts which may have fallen down during the winter are re-erected, bridges repaired, and generally the trail will be in its best state mid- to late summer.

Some slopes – such as boulderfields or avalanche slopes – do not lend themselves to a permanent trail. Often there are paint flashes to encourage walkers to all follow the same path so as to stabilise such slopes. The glacier section may be more or less snow-covered depending on how early it is in the summer season and how much snowfall there was late in the winter season.

Bad weather in the Alps can transform normally easy trails into stiff tests of navigation and tracking skills. The Tour of Monte Rosa is an Alpine trek which passes through some impressive ground, and should not be underestimated.

Footpaths and waymarks
Although most of the trails for the Tour of Monte Rosa are well used, you do need to use a map. Waymarking was, until recently, somewhat inconsistent. However, the last few years have seen a big push to sign the trail correctly on the Italian side, where it is now waymarked with yellow paint flashes. In Switzerland you will find the paths are generally waymarked with red and white paint flashes, indicating that it is a long-distance trek.

Nevertheless, the route is less obvious than some better-known treks such as the Tour of Mont Blanc. You cannot expect to step onto the path and just follow the paint flashes. This would be reckless and, surely, part of the fun of hiking is to use the map and decide which route to take. There are quite often route options, or you may decide you'd like to include a nearby summit or visit an interesting village. Equally some path junctions are not signed. Having said that, if you are looking to be on the main trail and the path you're on is very indistinct then you should check you haven't missed a turning.

Fog and snow can occur at any time in the Alps, and at such times those friendly little paint flashes tend to disappear. It is important to try to stay on the path, as the terrain 'off piste' tends to be very rough and difficult. In snow or bad visibility you will likely need to use map and compass (and maybe GPS if that's what you're used to).

The Italian maps often number footpaths, and although these numbers may correspond to numbers painted on the trail signs, don't bank on it. It's far better to use the map to see which direction a path should

The fabulous Höhenweg from Saas Fee to Grächen traversed on Stage 7 has some interesting sections along the way

(top) Follow the yellow brick road; (bottom) in the Italian part of the trek the Walser influence is evident on the signposts

take rather than trying to blindly follow unreliable numbers on the ground.

Splitting the tour into shorter sections

It is perfectly feasible to split the Tour of Monte Rosa into shorter sections, logically the Swiss section and the Italian section. Whichever option you choose make sure you don't finish your trek a long way from anywhere – for example, starting in Breuil-Cervinia and finishing in Macugnaga would mean a long and costly return to base. However, judicious use of some of the variants means that circuits can be worked out that finish in valleys where there is a reasonable transport option back to your starting point.

Swiss TMR
- Saas Fee to Grächen
- Grächen to Europahütte (check the feasibility of the Europaweg before setting out)
- Europahütte to Zermatt (check the feasibility of the Europaweg before setting out)
- Zermatt to Gandegghütte or Zermatt to Gornergrat – the latter end point gives good views of the Monte Rosa massif.

Italian TMR
- Breuil-Cervinia to Resy/St Jacques
- Resy/St Jacques to Gressoney St Jean
- Gressoney St Jean to Gabiet/ Orestes Hütte
- Gabiet/Orestes Hütte to Pastore/ Alagna
- Alagna/Pastore to Gressoney St Jean (by the alternative route) and bus back to Breuil-Cervinia.

Other walks in the area
There are a number of good walks that can be made from the main bases of Zermatt, Breuil-Cervinia, Saas Fee and Alagna. You will find guidebooks to local walks in these centres, and the tourist offices are always good sources of information on pleasant rest-day strolls or interesting explorations.

From Zermatt

- The Mettlehorn summit, accessed from Trift
- The villages of Winkelmatten and Findeln, then on up to Grindjsee and Sunnegga
- Höhbalmen (see Regional highlights)
- Trift (see Regional highlights)
- Hörnlihütte (see Regional highlights).

From Breuil-Cervinia

- The Lago Cignana, which can be reached via the Finestra di Cignana.
- The Rifugio Oriondé Duca Degli Abruzzi, for its proximity to the Matterhorn

A good walk from Saas Fee is the circuit up to Hannigalp.

From Alagna

The Glacier Trail, which is way-marked with information boards. It starts at the Acqua Bianca waterfall and goes as far as the Rifugio Crespi Calderini.

The circuit of paths joining the Orestes Hütte and Rifugio Pastore/Alagna can make for a good two-day outing, with great views of the high peaks.

Guided treks

The legal requirement to take people on guided treks on non-glaciated terrain in Europe is the diploma International Mountain Leader/Accompagnateur en Montagne (France/Switzerland/Italy). An unqualified person will not have liability insurance. These Guides are not only well qualified in navigation skills and the techniques for walking and leading groups, they are also a mine of information about the region, plants and flowers, wildlife, geology, history and culture. A day out with such a Guide should enhance your visit even if you can perfectly well find the path yourself.

For glaciated terrain a Guide must hold the UIAGM/IFMGA High Mountain diploma.

Most guided treks of the Tour will be led by an International Mountain Leader with a UIAGM/IFMAGA Guide for the glacier passage.

Hut contact details

Hut phone numbers and email addresses are given in Appendix C. While it is not necessary to book all your huts before starting out, it is advisable to book a day or two ahead, maybe more at a weekend. A completely booked trip may feel reassuring, but a day of bad weather or other changes of plan mean that it is necessary to rearrange all future bookings. Always call if you cannot get to a hut – it allows others to take the place, and avoids the hut initiating an expensive mountain rescue.

Other valley-based or hotel accommodation can be secured through the tourist offices (see Appendix D).

USING THIS GUIDE

This guide to the Tour of Monte Rosa is the result of several years' walking in the region. Use it as a tool to plan your trip. Once on the Tour a map, compass and willingness to adapt to conditions are all essential; the book is not enough on its own.

For this guide the 134km-long Tour has been divided into eight stages. These are **not** necessarily one-day stages, and some (for example Grächen to Zermatt) will be more comfortably achieved over two days or more. The route is described this way so as to give the individual the choice of how to plan the trek. Sometimes there is a wide choice of accommodation, at other times hardly any choice at all. Realistically you should allow 9–10 days to complete the Tour, so it is a suitable objective for a two-week break.

Each stage has an information box giving the details for the stage:
- starting and finishing points
- total ascent/descent, high point reached and distance in kilometres
- time
- maps needed
- facilities en route
- options for using transport (e.g. lifts or cable cars) to shorten or adapt the route
- accommodation
- extra information that may be pertinent.

Variants are also noted: this is a trek with many alternative ways, some of which are described as stage variants. Each stage also has escape routes briefly described, along with transport options for regaining the starting points. Accommodation is noted by name in the stage description, and further contact details are given in Appendix C.

Time for each stage is calculated roughly on the basis of climbing 300m every hour; the ascent time is halved for descent; where there are long flat sections these are calculated on a rate of 4km/hr. These times are given as a rough guide but should not be taken as anything other than that – they are not a challenge! Times are often noted on signposts in Switzerland and may vary from mine. Equally you may find your own times do not match mine (faster or slower) – after a day or so you'll have figured out your own rate of progress so adjust your planning accordingly.

The distance of a stage is difficult to calculate as there are often many zigzags on the ground that are not shown on the map. The distances given are therefore not exact.

Sketch maps accompany each stage. These are designed to show where the route goes and are based on the 1:50,000 map. Relevant details have been noted on the sketch map but these are not a substitute for the real thing. When walking this route you need to take the relevant sheet maps, and a compass, and to know how to use them.

The hills around Zermatt provide spectacular walking

Taking a break during the descent from the Colle del Turlo on Stage 5

Route profiles are provided to give an impression of the ups and downs encountered along the way.

In addition to the route description, this book also contains a fair amount of information about local history, culture and nature. While this information is not strictly necessary to do the trek, it is interesting to know a little more about the region you are visiting. You may only choose to read these sections when stuck in a hut on a wet afternoon with nothing else to read but a dog-eared out-of-date Alpine Club magazines in a language you don't understand!

The appendices contain a glossary of useful phrases and terms and the following additional information: a route summary table; a guide to the summits of the Monte Rosa massif; accommodation details; useful contacts (including tourist offices and Guides' offices, and travel companies); and a guide to glacier travel techniques. There are also suggestions for background reading. Information given was correct at the time of writing, but details do change and the latest ones can usually found by a quick internet search.

THE TOUR OF
MONTE ROSA

*Looking back at the huge southeast face of Monte Rosa from
Alpe Blatte, just above Rifugio Pastore (Stage 4)*

STAGE 1
Zermatt to Theodulpass

Start	Zermatt (1600m)
Finish	Theodulhütte (3317m)
Distance	11km
Total ascent	1701m
Total descent	0m
Time	6–7hrs
High point	(on foot) Theodulpass (3301m)
Maps	1:50,000 Carte Nationale de la Suisse 5006 Matterhorn Mischabel; 1:25,000 Carte Nationale de la Suisse 1348 Zermatt
Transport	Furi and Trockenersteg lifts or Klein Matterhorn lift
Access	To start: Train from Visp; bus and road access to Täsch, then train to Zermatt. To finish: Cable car from Breuil-Cervinia to Plateau Rosa, then on foot.
Accommodation	(on foot) Gandegghütte; Theodulhütte; (by lift) Rifugio Guide del Cervino; Theodulhütte
Variant	The only variant is to use the lifts. If you decide to take the Klein Matterhorn lift, the nearest accommodation is the Rifugio Guide del Cervino (3479m) at Testa Grigia, reached in about 40mins downhill walk on glacier from the lift. To reach the Theodulpass and Theodulhütte walk down the glacier for about 15mins more.
Facilities	Zermatt has everything anyone could ever desire. Theodulhütte at the Theodulpass; café and hut at Testa Grigia.
Escape route	None, other than to retrace your steps. If you encounter problems near a lift station you could use a lift to return to Zermatt.

If this is your first day walking in the Alps it will be a hard one. Not only is there a very big gain in altitude but you will also feel the effects of high altitude above about 3000m. It is highly recommended that you do a training day or two before starting the trek, or split the stage and stay at the Gandegghütte. Do not underestimate the rigours of the glacier passage at the end of the day when fatigue will make difficult conditions seem that much harder. Although the Theodulhütte is 'only' 2km up the glacier from where you leave the rocks after the Gandegghütte, the slope feels long and arduous. On the other hand, if you spend the night at Gandegg then you would be embarking on the glacier in the early morning, in which case it could be icy (see box on crossing the glacier).

Starting the trek in Zermatt allows the high summits of the Monte Rosa massif to be seen on the first day, a sight you'll want to savour – even though the actual peaks of Monte Rosa are just briefly visible from the glacier ascent. It's exciting trying to distinguish the different summits of the massif, acquainting yourself with the giants of Liskamm and the Breithorn, as well as the Mattertal peaks.

STARTING BY LIFT?

Several lifts lead out of Zermatt and you could take some (or all) to shorten the first day; perhaps to Trockenersteg and then continue on foot from there. However, I strongly recommend walking all the way from Zermatt to the Theodulpass. For one thing, a multi-day trek should really start on foot – not in a lift! In any case, the walk from Zermatt is very interesting and enjoyable and the lifts do not run directly above the walking route, making you feel that you might as well have hitched a ride.

Head out of Zermatt past the church and along the road towards the river. At a gravel works the road ends and a wide trail leads up towards Zmutt. Continue along the

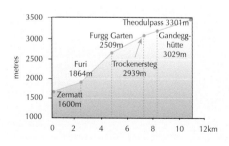

This is where Zermatt's most famous Mountain Guide, Ulrich Innerbinen, passed his summers, and you can see the boulder where he and his sisters practised climbing in the meadows.

river until a sign indicates the trail up to Blatten and Furi, which stays more or less under the cables of the Furi cable car. Blatten is a charming village with a beautifully restored white chapel. The old wooden chalets are evidence of a simpler time when local families headed up to these summer farms to graze their animals in the meadows and to grow food for the hard winter months. ◄

From Blatten the trail meanders through larch forest to arrive at the hamlet of **Furi**, home to several cafés and the lift station.

From Furi follow the signs towards Furgg. The path begins on rough ski pistes, but the higher you go the more pleasant it becomes. The trail heads around towards Hermettji then back across the hillside to cross the Furggbach river.

> As height is gained take the time to stop and look around; this climb gives a good opportunity to get to know the **surrounding peaks**. Behind you to the west of the Mattertal are particularly fine views of the Obergabelhorn, Weisshorn and Zinal Rothorn, and to the east of the valley are the Dom and Täschhorn. To the southeast you can make out the long Gornergletscher snaking down to Zermatt.

At times the path is well marked with red and white flashes, at other times less clearly, but there are useful signposts every so often (and if all else fails the big cable car up to **Trockenersteg** is hard to miss over on your left). Eventually grassy slopes give way to rockier terrain and a final climb leads to Trockenersteg lift station.

> In winter this area is buried under a forgiving mantle of snow, but in the summer, once the snow has melted, it is quite frankly a bit of a mess. Probably when they have finished the **ski resort development** it will be landscaped and improved.

There is a café here, but unless you're desperate continue on for another 15mins to the **Gandegghütte**,

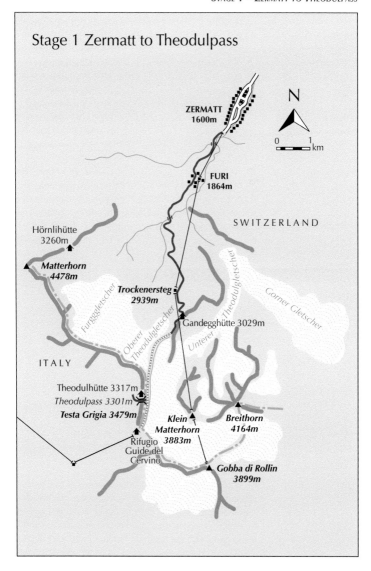

Stage 1 Zermatt to Theodulpass

ZERMATT
1600m

N

0   1
km

FURI
1864m

SWITZERLAND

Hörnlihütte
3260m

▲ *Matterhorn*
4478m

Furggletscher

Trockenersteg
2939m

Gandegghütte 3029m

Oberer Theodulgletscher

Unterer Theodulgletscher

Gorner Gletscher

ITALY

Theodulhütte 3317m
Theodulpass 3301m
Testa Grigia 3479m

▲ *Klein Matterhorn*
3883m

▲ *Breithorn*
4164m

Rifugio
Guide del
Cervino

▲ *Gobba di Rollin*
3899m

reached by following a clear flashed path along rocky slabs.

> This restaurant and typical **Swiss mountain hut** occupies a privileged position high above the Unterer Theodule Glacier with fabulous views of the Zermatt peaks. It's a real delight, complete with flags and geraniums and a wonderful sunny terrace. Find yourself a table, order a big lunch and savour that view – it's what you came for.

When you're stuffed full of cheese and chocolate it's time to consider the rest of the day's programme. The route onwards from Gandegg is glaciated, and follows a summer ski piste up the **Oberer Theodulegletscher**. This is the only glacier passage on the Tour of Monte Rosa and the degree of difficulty encountered varies from one extreme to the other.

CROSSING THE GLACIER

Don't be surprised to see people walking on the ski piste in all sorts of attire, from town shoes to running gear to full-blown mountaineering kit. You must make your own decision as to how to deal with this section. Take note of the following:

- there are crevasses on this slope and these are dangerous, especially if you fall into one unroped
- the glacier will generally be icier early in the day, getting softer later, but on cloudy or windy days the snow may not melt noticeably at all
- July usually has more snow cover than August
- the only safe way to walk on a snow-covered glacier is to rope up, and to have practised glacier-travel techniques in advance.

The trail is marked onwards over the rocks and around onto the glacier. Once embarked on the glacier it is a question of finding the best route. In good firm snow it's quite easy; just keep to the side of the ski piste, starting on the true right bank of the glacier (left as you walk up) then heading across to the true left bank (right walking up) as soon as possible. When there is lit-tle snow cover it will be icy and/or wet. Try to avoid the water channels and make the best use of gravel on the surface, heading south and up towards the flat plateau at the **Theodulpass**. ▶

Once at the Theodulpass the **Theodulhütte** is obvi-ous just above to the northwest. You will probably arrive here a little late in the day to descend to Breuil-Cervinia, and far too late to continue on round to St Jacques at the end of Stage 2.

> The **Theodulhütte** is a good place to spend the night if you want to savour being high up in the mountains. The Theodulpass is a historic spot, and to get a real feel for this you'll want to linger when all the skiers and tourists go back down to the val-ley. The hut has been renovated but the old dining room and bedrooms remain and spending a night there is a great experience.

Be aware that skiers will descend at speed. They do not expect to find hikers in their way; respect the fact that this is a ski area and stay well to the side.

Sunrise on Mont Blanc, seen from the Rifugio Guide del Cervino

THE BREITHORN

En route for the Breithorn summit, an optional extra for the equipped and strong trekker

The Tour of Monte Rosa takes you very near to the Breithorn peak so you may want to consider it as an optional extra during or after the Tour. 'Wide mountain' would be the literal translation, and it fits this summit well: the Breithorn stretches over 2km from its main western summit to the eastern one. Its huge bulk towers above Zermatt, and can be seen when coming up the Mattertal well before the Matterhorn deigns to show itself.

At 4164m the Breithorn is not the highest peak in the area but it must be the most climbed due to its accessibility from the Klein Matterhorn lift and the relative ease of the ascent from the south side. It is the most westerly peak of the giants rising up from the Gorner Glacier. The Breithorn has four summits: the westerly high point, the central summit (4160m), the eastern summit (4141m) and Roccia Nera (4075m) which – as its name suggests – is a rocky summit above the Schwarztor col separating it from Pollux.

The North Face is steep, complex and avalanche prone, and when viewed from that side the Breithorn seems an impossible challenge to those aspirant climbers who ascend this as their first 4000m peak. In total contrast the southern side presents a gentle snow slope which allows the ascent to be achieved in about 3hrs from the Klein Matterhorn cable car. The Breithorn was first climbed by this route in 1813 when it was somewhat more of an endeavour without the aid of lifts. From Italy the Testa Grigia lift gives convenient access, but this entails an hour's more climbing.

Be prepared to see people in all sorts of gear ranging from ultra-cool latest fashion designer shoes to jeans and T-shirts to well-equipped mountaineers. You'll probably see people on skis going up too. Do not be misled by the unroped folk who look like they've just nipped up in between shopping in Zermatt. **This is a glacier and there are crevasses.** You do need to be roped up for the ascent and you will almost certainly need to use crampons. Take a Guide if you are not versed in glacier-travel techniques. While the ascent seems pretty innocuous in sunny weather and good snow conditions, it is a whole different ball game in the fog when navigation can be very difficult. Five ski tourers died here in 1977.

The Breithorn rises to 4164m, and for many people this will be the first time they have reached that altitude so the risk of High Mountain Sickness makes it difficult to place the ascent of the Breithorn during the Tour of Monte Rosa as described here. To do it en route from the Theodulpass means that it will fall on your second day when you will hardly be acclimatised. It's probably better to climb the summit after the trek, doing it in a day from Zermatt by taking the Klein Matterhorn cable car first thing in the morning.

At any time during the summer there will be lots of guided groups, as the Breithorn is bread-and-butter work for the Guides from Zermatt and Breuil-Cervinia and they do an excellent job. A guided ascent will not only keep you safe but the Guide will also be able to tell you about all the surrounding peaks. It is truly a 360-degree panorama: from the Matterhorn to the Dent Blanche to the Obergabelhorn, the Zinal Rothorn and the Weisshorn guarding the Mattertal to the Dom and the Täschhorn and the Monte Rosa massif. Nearer are the twin peaks of Pollux and Castor, and far away in the mist the distant Italian plains.

The Theodulhütte and the Matterhorn

If you plan to descend to Plan Maison/Breuil-Cervinia check the time of the last lift down from Testa Grigia (it will be mid-afternoon) so you know how long you have to enjoy the views en route.

A further 1km along the glacier will get you to **Testa Grigia** where you'll find the **Rifugio Guide del Cervino** and the cable car down to Plan Maison and Breuil-Cervinia. This plateau area is referred to as Plateau Rosa on all the ski lift information. ◄

You could equally well spend the night at **Rifugio Guide del Cervino**; it puts you a little nearer to the Breithorn. However, unless you were already acclimatised before you started the Tour it is not recommended that you attempt the 4164m Breithorn on your second day because of the risk of High Mountain Sickness. Better to do it from Zermatt at the end of the Tour as a separate excursion.

STAGE 2
Theodulpass to Resy/St Jacques

Start	Theodulhütte (3317m)
Finish	Resy (2072m); or St Jacques (1689m)
Distance	14km; or 14.5km to St Jacques
Total ascent	351m; or 151m to St Jacques
Total descent	1580m; or 1779 to St Jacques
Time	5hrs
High point	Theodulpass (3301m)
Maps	1:50,000 IGC 5 Cervino-Matterhorn e Monte Rosa; 1:25,000 IGC 108 Cervino Matterhorn Breuil-Cervinia Champoluc
Transport	Cable car from Testa Grigia to Plan Maison or Cime Bianche station
Access	To start: Cable cars from Breuil-Cervinia or Zermatt will take you to within 15mins–1hr of the pass; then on foot on glacier. To finish: Resy is accessed by a steep footpath heading east from the centre of St Jacques; St Jacques is reached by road from the main Aosta Valley, taking the Ayas Valley via Verrès, Brusson and Champoluc.

Accommodation	Breuil-Cervinia has several hotels; Rifugio GB Ferraro; Rifugio Guide di Frachey; St Jacques has a few hotels
Variant	The main alternative for this stage involves walking up to Testa Grigia and taking the cable car to Cime Bianche station, Plan Maison, or even all the way to Breuil-Cervinia (and back up to Cime Bianche to continue). However, once over the Colle Supérieure delle Cime Bianche there is no alternative route until the end of the day when you must decide whether to go up to Resy or down to St Jacques.
Warning	Do not underestimate this stage if you are tackling it in a clockwise direction. If it is late in the day when you reach the Colle Supérieure delle Cime Bianche then consider descending and staying at Breuil-Cervinia. The last cable car up from Breuil-Cervinia to Plateau Rosa (Testa Grigia) is mid-afternoon, earlier than you'd expect.
Facilities	St Jacques is a small village with just a shop and hotels. Resy comprises two refuges and a few other buildings. You can buy basic snacks and a picnic for the next day.
Escape route	You can take the lift down to Breuil-Cervinia, then catch a bus down the valley to the main Aosta Valley. From here a long bus route via the Grand St Bernard Tunnel will get you back to Switzerland. Alternatively you could take the lifts back up to Testa Grigia and return to Zermatt by the Klein Matterhorn lift. Bear in mind, however, that you do have to walk uphill on the glacier between the two lifts. It is easier to descend the ski piste down the Oberer Theodulegletscher to Trockensteg then take the lift down to Zermatt.

The route described is the shortest way down from the Theodulpass and to the upper Ayas Valley. It does not take in Breuil-Cervinia. However, there is nothing to stop you descending to the town and then picking up the route again from Plan Maison or the higher Cime Bianche cable car station.

Centuries ago the **Theodulpass** formed a much-used passage from what are now the Italian valleys to Switzerland. Such passes were used by

The Theodulpass is one of the oldest crossing places in the Alps. If the slopes are snow-free it's not too difficult to descend from the pass. The path is relatively easy to make out and there is the interesting Cappella Bontadini to visit and great views of the Italian face of the Matterhorn (El Cervino). From the Cime Bianche cable car station a trail heads straight across to the Colle Supérieure delle Cime Bianche. Once over this pass you enter one of the most beautiful and wild valleys imaginable. This valley is reached by a well-made path which leads down under the hanging seracs of the Ventina Glacier to the icy blue Gran Lago, before descending once again, to the rustic Alpe Mase. From here you climb up to Resy on the official Tour, or, alternatively, go down to St Jacques for the night.

traders, smugglers, immigrants, armies and farmers. Artefacts found here show the pass was used during Roman times, and we can only assume that the terrain was somewhat different from that encountered today. The climate in those days was considerably warmer and so the pass would not have been glaciated. However, there were still many risks to be faced: bad weather, attack, disorientation and fatigue, to mention just a few.

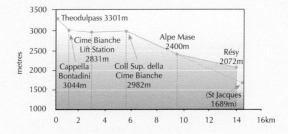

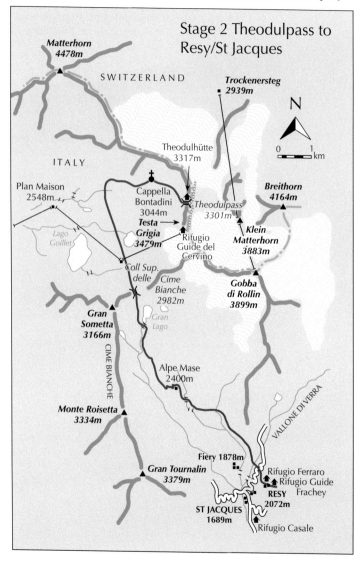

Stage 2 Theodulpass to Resy/St Jacques

Descent to Colle Supérieure delle Cime Bianche in snow
If there is snow on the slopes below the Theodulpass to
Plan Maison do not descend on foot. If the snow is fresh
it can be difficult to find the path. This is equally the case
with névé, with the additional problem that early in the
morning the névé will probably be icy, and later in the
day it may become slushy. Walk the kilometre up to the
Testa Grigia cable car station and take a lift down, at
least to the first station (Cime Bianche), then head across
to the Colle Supérieure delle Cime Bianche. Sometimes
it's easier to go down to Plan Maison then walk across
and up to the Colle, avoiding some snowy traverses.

From the **Theodulpass** the path heads down westwards,
soon passing an iron cross. There are waymarks from
time to time of varying colours; occasionally the TMR is
marked in reassuring yellow diamonds.

Do not expect to find the **wilderness** encountered
by early travellers. These slopes have been 'raped
and pillaged' in the interests of skiing: bulldozed
ski pistes and lift stations along with associated
junk are the order of the day. However, there is so
much beauty all around, you can ignore the ski pistes. Alpine flowers abound and ibex are often to be
seen.

After descending for about 15mins pick up a trail
heading right (northwest). Despite the numerous tracks
and pistes, in good visibility your objective will be clear:
the first station of the cable car which descends from
Testa Grigia. However, the trail does not go there directly.
It heads across to the winter ski lift which serves the
Theodulpass. Here at 3044m you'll find a cluster of lift
buildings and the **Cappella Bontadini**.

Bontadini was an Italian alpinist and there is a
memorial plaque for him in the tiny chapel sand-
wiched between the lift buildings – a delightful
juxtaposition of old and new. An information board

here states, 'The landscape in front of you wasn't always as you see it today…' Too true! Presumably travellers stopped at the chapel to pray for protection before tackling the final climb to the pass; now it's a storehouse for rescue equipment. Try hard and you might get an inkling of the trepidation felt by those travellers of old…

From here the TMR is signposted across the hillside heading south. Be sure not to miss the route. Take the narrow flat trail across shaly slopes to the **Cime Bianche station** of the Testa Grigia (Plateau Rosa) cable car (2831m) next to the Cime Bianche lake. ▶ The path is signed with yellow flashes, notably on pylons, and goes around the slopes heading for the **Colle Supérieure delle Cime Bianche**.

Enjoy the views of the Matterhorn – you won't see it again until you return to Zermatt. At 2982m the col really is a fine **vantage point**: from the summits

In fog navigation will be tricky here as there are few features in this area except man-made ski tracks and associated shacks and cables.

The wild and barren slopes of the Colle Supérieure delle Cime Bianche

above Breuil-Cervinia to the hanging ice field of the Ventina Glacier to the unusual pale orange limestone formations which form the Cime Bianche ridge.

The mechanics of the ski resorts are now left behind as you enter the wonderful Ventina or Rollin Valley (the map does not give a precise name).

This valley is like a **different world**: rarely will you see more than a handful of walkers here, the slopes are flowery and lush, the lakes deep azure, sometimes frozen, sometimes home to birds, often giving beautiful reflections of the surrounding rocky peaks.

Take your time as you descend steeply via well-made zigzags to the **Gran Lago**, a good place for a break as you acclimatise to the wild and silent surroundings. The way is now fairly gentle and you can enjoy the views. To the west are the impressive multi-coloured limestone cliffs of Monte Roisetta and the Grand Tournalin, and soon the basic but lived-in farm at **Alpe Mase** (2400m) is reached. Making a living here, albeit just for the summer, must be a fairly harsh business.

Below, the path ambles along next to the grassy-banked stream, weaving in and out of boulders. The map shows a choice of paths here but there seems to be one main one, well signed with yellow paint flashes. Cotton grass, orchids, gentians, hawksbeard and many other flowers abound according to the season. Eventually a ruin is passed and a signpost shows a footpath junction.

Take the leftwards trail towards Resy. The small path leaves the Ventina Valley over a small col and descends into another equally idyllic flat valley defined by a lovely stream. Ahead are views of distant peaks. Eventually the path steepens with big rocky steps as it follows the route of the stream, which at this point becomes a gushing waterfall. The town of Champoluc can be seen way below in the Ayas Valley. Soon the treeline is reached and the trail goes left then right with a short ascent leading to

Descending from the Colle Supérieure delle Cima Bianche

a junction with a wide track in a large clearing. Go right along this broad track until a footpath is signed off left into the forest. This trail goes on up to **Resy**, arriving at the Rifugio GB Ferraro. The Rifugio Guide di Frachey is just below. ▶

The snowy peaks make a reappearance, with the wide ridge of the Breithorn on the left, Pollux and Castor on the right.

Resy occupies a commanding position perched high above the valley on south-facing slopes. At 2072m this was once one of the highest villages to be inhabited year-round. The slopes were previously glaciated and the moraine deposits make for a very fertile soil; the main crops were cereals (rye and barley), beans, cabbage and turnips. Later potatoes were grown. Now there is far less farming as

There are two huts in the hamlet of Resy, occupying a fine position high above the Ayas Valley

CHAMOIS

Chamois are quite timid and will usually run away when they spot you

The chamois is particularly well adapted to life in the mountains. Its mistrust and flair enable it to avoid most predators; its robust disposition means it can survive the rigorous winters; its physical agility and 'gripping' hooves enable it to move easily on the most difficult terrain. With a perfectly proportioned body, slim and graceful, the chamois is probably the most elegant of Alpine mammals.

Often misidentified as a deer, the chamois is actually a deer/goat hybrid. In the summer its fur is short, light grey or yellow beige, with a dark stripe along the back. The coat thickens and turns black in winter. Its face is light coloured with a darker muzzle; both male and female have short horns with a pronounced backwards curve. At first glance it is difficult to differentiate between males and females, although the latter are slightly smaller and less sturdy.

Chamois are gregarious creatures and will usually be seen in groups. They give birth in late May or early June, to allow time for the young to become strong before the winter sets in. During the winter months chamois survive by reducing their movements to a minimum and eating whatever vegetation is not covered by snow, favouring wind-blown arêtes and slopes that have avalanched.

Although often associated with the precipitous rocky terrain of the higher slopes, the chamois seems to prefer the forests but has been forced to occupy ever-higher ground due to increasing human population of the Alpine valleys. They have few natural enemies but there is a permitted hunting quota. When alarmed the chamois emits a short sound like a whistle to alert the whole herd, which flees across the hillside.

Redstarts are one of the smaller birds to be seen flitting amongst the rocks

tourism has provided an easier way to make a living, and Resy is mainly just inhabited in the summer. An evening spent here watching the sun set over the far-distant Aosta Valley is an unforgettable experience.

There are two refuges here: the **Rifugio Guide di Frachey** and, just above, the **Rifugio GB Ferraro**, named after a local alpinist who died in the mountains in 1931. The refuge opened the year after his death and provides an excellent stopover in all respects.

Alternative finish at St Jacques

From the footpath junction below Alpe Mase, the trail going straight ahead descends to the hamlet of **Fiery** (1878m), which used to be a military post, and onwards through forest to reach the road not far from **St Jacques**. Take this if you need supplies or a hotel (rather than a refuge) – reascending next day to continue from Resy – or if you are planning to follow Stage 3A.

STAGE 3
Resy/St Jacques to Gabiet

Start	Resy (2072m); or St Jacques (1689m)
Finish	Gabiet (2342m)
Distance	10km; or 10.5km from St Jacques; 10km via Passo del Rothorn
Total ascent	1119m; or 1319m from St Jacques; 1000m via Passo del Rothorn
Total descent	850m; 866m via Passo del Rothorn
Time	5hrs 30mins–6hrs; or 6–6hrs 30mins from St Jacques; 6hrs via Passo del Rothorn
High point	2672m
Maps	1:50,000 IGC 5 Cervino-Matterhorn e Monte Rosa; 1:25,000 109 Monte Rosa Alagna Macugnaga Gressoney; IGC 108 Cervino Matterhorn Breuil-Cervinia Champoluc
Transport	Lifts from Bettaforca to Stafal, Stafal to Gabiet
Access	To start: Road access from the Aosta Valley to St Jacques; Resy must be accessed on foot. To finish: By ski lifts or on foot.
Accommodation	Albergo del Ponte; Rifugio Gabiet; Orestes Hütte
Notes	Most maintenance work on ski lifts and the pistes is done during the summer months and footpaths may be disturbed during such work. Do not be surprised to find the lifts are closed for 1½–2hrs between midday and 2pm.
Variants	To avoid the Bettaforca ski area, you could detour over the Passo del Rothorn but the route is poorly marked and not advisable in fog.
Facilities	St Jacques has a small shop and a few hotels. Bars at Bettaforca, Sant'Anna, Stafal and Gabiet (Albergo Ponte and Rifugio del Lys – this latter is now just a café with no overnight accommodation) and at the Gabiet Lake (Rifugio Gabiet).
Escape route	Any problems encountered during this stage would require a descent to the nearest valley – either the Ayas Valley or the Lys Valley. There are regular bus services down to the Aosta Valley from where transport can be taken around to Switzerland via the Grand St Bernard Tunnel.

The section from Resy to Gabiet by the regular TMR route is basically contained in the Gressoney ski area and could be done almost entirely on lifts. If time is limited you could walk from Resy up to the Bettaforca Pass, then take the chairlift down to Sant'Anna and the Stafal-Sant'Anna cable car to Stafal. From here a cable car takes you up the other side of the valley to Gabiet where there are two accommodation options. Alternatively you could take the next cable car up to the Paso dei Salati above the Col d'Olen and continue on foot down to Alagna or the Rifugio Pastore the same day.

However, assuming time is not an issue there is plenty of good walking to be enjoyed on this section to Gabiet, either by the regular route or the variant over the Passo del Rothorn. The main route goes over Bettaforca then down a trail that cuts the ski pistes to Sant'Anna. An easy path then descends in forest to Stafal. On the other side the trail ambles along by the river before climbing up through meadows to the first cable car station with the Albergo del Ponte just above. Just around the corner to the south is the Gabiet Lake and refuge.

▶ From Resy follow the road which goes east, past a tiny pond surrounded by willowherb. Views from here down towards the Ayas Valley are spectacular. The road continues, meeting an attractive stream.

Variant over the Passo del Rothorn
There is an option here to get to Stafal over the Passo del Rothorn and avoid the Bettaforca ski area. The TMR map shows this as a glaciated route but there is no longer a glacier here. However, the path is poorly marked towards the top – so not a good choice for foggy weather.

If you finished the previous stage at St Jacques, look for a steep footpath heading east from the town centre to Resy.

Elevation profile: Résy 2072m, Colle di Bettaforca 2672m, Sant'Anna 2172m, Stafal 1823m, Gabiet 2342m, St Jacques 1689m. Vertical axis: metres (1000–3500). Horizontal axis: 0–12km.

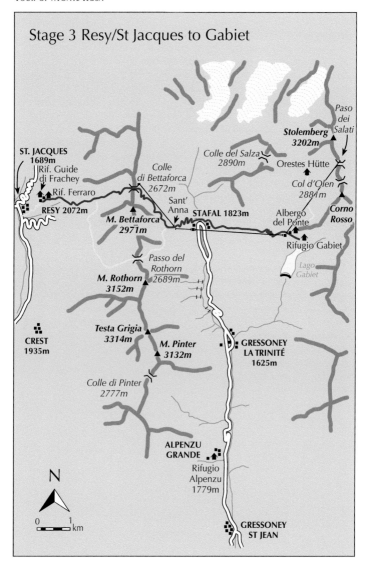

Stage 3 Resy/St Jacques to Gabiet

From Resy the walk is rather long and tedious on forest tracks until above the treeline when the trail becomes a lot more scenic. Towards the pass the path loses itself somewhat in boulders and is poorly marked. Once over the **Passo del Rothorn** (2689m) the onwards path is good, leading past a couple of small lakes, and the views of the glaciated peaks are very fine. A quick descent leads to the Sant'Anna mid station (2172m) from where you can either continue down the path to **Stafal** as described in the regular route, or hop on the cable car.

Taking a rest to admire the Monte Rosa massif en route to the Pass del Rothorn

About 20mins after the turnoff to the pass a footpath goes off left, taking a direct line up a rounded shoulder, following right underneath a chair lift (sometimes running in summer). ▸ The easier option is to follow the wide track all the way to the **Colle di Bettaforca** (2672m).

This is a good route if you've had enough of zigzags, but it could be a somewhat brutal warm-up first thing in the morning.

Looking back you can just make out Resy on the shoulder of the hillside. But new vistas await, notably the peaks of the **Lys Valley**, best known of which is Liskamm or Lyskamm. Just above the col, to the north, is the top of the chairlift, which usually runs

89

up from Sant'Anna and the Stafal cable car during the summer.

There is a well situated café restaurant right at the top of this lift and often ibex roam around the nearby slopes. There are also lots of Alpine flowers to be seen near the col, notably alpine toadflax, whose tiny purple and orange flowers seem to favour such shaly ground.

The trail down from the Bettaforca Pass more or less follows underneath this lift and is waymarked in yellow.

This is marmot territory and your descent will almost certainly be greeted with shrieking whistles from furry chaps who've spotted you. On their summer 'all you can eat' programme marmots need to consume 400g of greens at every meal, adding a bit of variety with insects such as larvae or grasshoppers. An afternoon siesta helps the digestive process before the evening gastronomic extravaganza, and they are often seen soaking up the rays on flat rocks during this part of the day.

At Sant'Anna there is another café and this part of the hike could easily turn into a café to café extravaganza! Either take the cable car on down from here or follow the wide track that descends through patchy forest to the big car park and lift station at **Stafal**, where there yet more cafés to tempt you. ◄

A regular shuttle bus runs between Stafal and Gressoney when the lifts are open.

The route onwards heads into the Gressoney lift system. However, although there are still cable cars overhead, the trail up the Vallone di Mos to the middle station (Gabiet) is very pleasant. To find the path, cross the road from the Stafal lift station and follow a small road uphill until you meet the footpath on the right, signed as TMR. This goes into larch forest alongside a river which it crosses a couple of times, then begins quite a steep climb to the top of the first cable car. This section of hillside is sometimes disturbed by work on the ski pistes but in general the path is easy to follow.

Head of the Lys Valley

The climb is relatively gentle and leads to the middle station of the cable car, known as **Gabiet** (2342m).

There are two possibilities for accommodation in the immediate vicinity of **Gabiet**. Firstly the rather fine Albergo del Ponte, more of a hotel than a hut, and a popular lunch venue during the summer season.

Just few minutes' walk to the south takes you to the Gabiet Lake. The attractiveness of this lake depends on how much water it holds (it is dammed and thus the level changes radically), but when it's full it's very pretty. On the far side of the lake is the Rifugio Gabiet, offering traditional accommodation in small rooms with a Walser theme.

Once evening comes you'll begin to feel like you're in a wild mountain environment again. The icy slopes of Liskamm can be seen towering overhead, while to the south are the seemingly endless rocky peaks which turn a rosy pink as darkness falls.

HUTS AND HOW THINGS CAN CHANGE

Until 2011 if there was one hut not to be missed on the Tour of Monte Rosa it was the Rifugio Guglielmina, which dated from 1878 when Giuseppe Guglielmina built it as an intermediate hostel for those tackling the long stage from Alagna to the Gnifetti hut in the days before cable cars.

Five years of work produced the Hotel Guglielmina, billed as the highest hotel in Europe. The hotel soon attracted a large and famous clientele, including Queen Margherita of Italy and many well-known British people, alpinists and otherwise. The hotel was enlarged in 1930 and again in 1950. Each day a mule service from Alagna ensured that guests could walk up and have their luggage taken up in advance. The mules also transported bread, clean linen and the mail, among other necessities. This was a smart hotel for the discerning traveller – white-gloved servants waited on the guests, and Guides were on call for those with aspirations to go higher. Monte Rosa became a common objective.

After a period of closure the building was renovated and reopened in the 1990s as a mountain hut and also a ski bar, being right next to the Gressoney ski pistes. For 20 years Guglielmina was an extremely popular place to stay for hikers and skiers alike. Sadly the building was destroyed by a catastrophic fire on 23 December 2011.

While wishing to preserve the memory of this old lodging I also include this account to show that even in the mountains things change: huts close, huts open (notably the new Orestes Hütte), huts get damaged, huts are renovated. At the time of writing there are no huts open on the Col d'Olen – in fact several huts in this area, including the substantial Rifugio Città di Vigevano, are closed with no predicted opening date and are therefore not suggested as stopovers for the trek. In the future this could change and you may find newly opened huts along the trail and wonder why they were not mentioned here.

When planning your trek do check that your planned stopovers are open. At the very least call the night before to make sure there is space for you (and if you have booked then change your route be sure to also call to cancel). If you find a new hut en route then stop by and have a cappuccino and treat it as a bonus!

Extension to the Orestes Hütte

There is a third accommodation option. The **Orestes Hütte** (2600m) is relatively new and doesn't appear on the maps at the time of writing. Although slightly off the official TMR trail, this hut merits the detour for its fine regional food and the possibility of small rooms for a night of comfort, albeit at a slightly higher price.

It can be reached in 1hr further walk uphill from Gabiet. Follow the yellow waymarks of the TMB trail to about 2500m where a trail branches off left (north) leading to the hut at 2600m. Allow about 1hr 15mins from the Orestes Hütte back onto the TMR trail at the Col d'Olen for the next stage. ▸

The Orestes Hütte enjoys a commanding position above the Gressoney Valley (photo courtesy of the Orestes Hütte)

For an alternative route from St Jacques to the Orestes Hütte via Colle di Pinter see Stage 3A.

STAGE 3A
St Jacques to Gabiet via Colle di Pinter

Start	St Jacques (1689m)
Finish	Gabiet (2342m); or the Orestes Hütte (2600m)
Distance	20km; 22.5km to the Orestes Hütte
Total ascent	1805m; 2063m to the Orestes Hütte
Total descent	1152m
Time	12hrs; 13hrs to the Orestes Hütte
High point	Colle di Pinter (2777m)
Maps	1:50,000 IGC 5 Cervino-Matterhorn e Monte Rosa; 1:25,000 109 Monte Rosa Alagna Macugnaga Gressoney; IGC 108 Cervino Matterhorn Breuil-Cervinia Champoluc
Transport	Lift from Stafal to Gabiet
Access	To start: Road access from the Aosta Valley to St Jacques. To finish: By ski lifts or on foot.
Accommodation	Rifugio Alpenzu; Gressoney la Trinité has one or two hotels, Gressoney St Jean has many more; Albergo del Ponte; Rifugio Gabiet; Orestes Hütte
Variants	If you want to walk the main TMR route to Gabiet, then you can follow the route described for Orestes Hütte as far as Stafal and then turn east on the TMR.
Facilities	St Jacques has a small shop and a few hotels. Gressoney la Trinité has a shop, but Gressoney St Jean (off route to the south) is a better source for supplies. Bar at Gabiet.
Escape route	Any problems encountered during this stage would require a descent to the nearest valley – either the Ayas Valley or the Lys Valley. There are regular bus services down to the Aosta Valley from where transport can be taken around to Switzerland via the Grand St Bernard Tunnel.

From St Jacques this trail traverses the hillside as far as Champoluc and then the route goes up the Cuneaz Valley to the Colle di Pinter. This a wild, almost barren area, but down the other side you reach the Alpine meadows and summer farm of Alpenzu, a gem that deserves a visit, and a night (if you have the time) at the delightful refuge. There are no ski lifts at all in this area, which gives a wonderful remote feeling of wilderness.

A trail around the hillside, the Walserweg, provides a beautiful route to Gressoney la Trinité. From here the main route heads north-east towards Lago Gabiet. Alternatively, you can walk a couple of kilometres up the road or take the bus to reach Stafal. From here you can either rejoin the route of Stage 3 to Gabiet, or avoid the ski area by taking the trail up the Salza Valley from Stafal to stay at the Orestes Hütte. Whichever option you choose, this stage would make a long day so a night either at Alpenzu or at Gressoney on the way is recommended.

Leave **St Jacques** on the well-marked path, which heads east up the hill to Alpe Ciacerio at 1975m, then takes a balcony route southwards all the way along to the hamlet of **Crest** (1935m), above Champoluc, passing several ski lifts in the process.

A beautiful fresco in St Jacques

The path regains its easterly direction to enter the Cuneaz Valley and climbs fairly steadily, well above the treeline with fine views below and across the Ayas Valley. The terrain becomes more barren and rocky, with a couple of small lakes just before the **Colle di Pinter** (2777m).

This is a fabulous **viewpoint** – Monte Pinter (3132m) is just up on the left and those with lots of energy and time might be tempted by this scramble. The tiny Lateltin bivouac hut and be seen perched on the rocky shoulder, but probably best to press on to more salubrious accommodation.

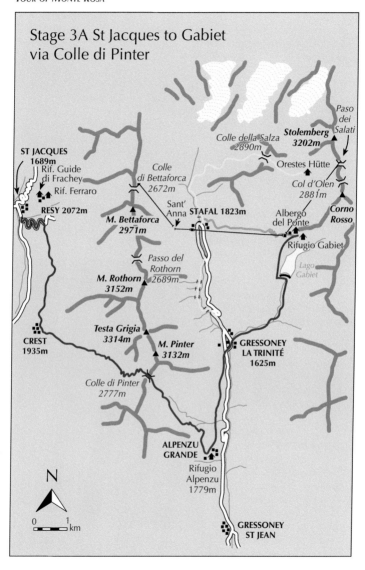

Stage 3A St Jacques to Gabiet
via Colle di Pinter

Paso dei Salati

Colle della Salza 2890m

Stolemberg 3202m

ST JACQUES 1689m
Rif. Guide di Frachey
Rif. Ferraro

RESY 2072m

Colle di Bettaforca 2672m

Sant' Anna

STAFAL 1823m

Orestes Hütte

Col d'Olen 2881m

Corno Rosso

Albergo del Ponte

Rifugio Gabiet

Lago Gabiet

M. Bettaforca 2971m

Passo del Rothorn 2689m

M. Rothorn 3152m

Testa Grigia 3314m

M. Pinter 3132m

CREST 1935m

GRESSONEY LA TRINITÉ 1625m

Colle di Pinter 2777m

ALPENZU GRANDE

Rifugio Alpenzu 1779m

N

0   1 km

GRESSONEY ST JEAN

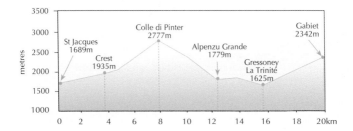

Descending towards Alpenzu, the Monte Rosa massif and associated summits can be seen way up the Lys Valley providing anticipation of more mountain vistas to come over the next days. Passing the ancient farm buildings of Alpe Loage the trail continues its descent to reach **Alpenzu** on the edge of the forest.

It would be hard to resist an overnight at the charming Rifugio Alpenzu

The village of **Alpenzu** (1780m) is the site of one of the oldest Walser settlements, a German-speaking community which originated in the Swiss Valais. Documents record that a village of sorts has existed on this site since the 13th century. This cluster of 13 wooden chalets, which has remained practically intact since 1668, sits on a rocky promontory, a natural balcony with a remarkable view of the Monte Rosa massif and of the Lys Valley. The Rifugio Alpenzu has been lovingly restored and provides very comfortable accommodation, both in dormitories and en suite bedrooms. Advance reservation is strongly recommended.

From the hamlet a good trail, the Walser Way, heads north, holding a fairly steady line along the edge of the forest, to come out at **Gressoney la Trinité**.

The best way from here to reach Gabiet is to take the path directly out of the village, heading north-east (this path is signed number 4). This starts as an ancient mule trail up to the higher meadows and initially winds

Gabiet Lake above Gressoney

its way quite steeply past a few old farm buildings, following the true left bank of the stream, crossing briefly
over to the right then finally deciding left is best and staying on that side for much of the ascent. Once the stream
crossings are done the route up the Ruesso Valley is just
fabulous, very quiet among meadow flowers with lovely
background views.

Higher up the ground steepens, the stream divides
and there is some rocky ground to be dealt with before
reaching the **Lago Gabiet**. Right up under the dam the
path goes out left up rocks and finds its way over the edge
of the dam by a narrow traverse. ▶ The **Rifugio Gabiet** is
clearly seen on the far (eastern) side of the lake.

If the lake is full it
will look beautiful in
the sunshine. If not
it can look a mess.

There are two possibilities for **accommodation**
in the immediate vicinity. Firstly the rather fine
Albergo del Ponte, at the top of the cable car station
at Gabiet. This is more of a hotel than a hut, and
a popular lunch venue during the summer season.

Just a few minutes' walk on round the lake
takes you to the Rifugio Gabiet which offers traditional accommodation in small rooms with a
Walser theme.

To the Orestes Hütte via Stafal
From Gressoney La Trinité, walk a couple of kilometres
up the road or take the bus to reach **Stafal**.

At Stafal you could join the **main TMR route** to
Gabiet. The route onwards heads into the Gressoney
lift system but the trail up the Vallone di Mos to the
middle station (Gabiet) is very pleasant. To find the
path, cross the road from the lift station and follow
a small road uphill until you meet the footpath on
the right, signed as TMR. This goes into larch forest
alongside a river which it crosses a couple of times,
then begins quite a steep climb to the top of the
first cable car. This section of hillside is sometimes
disturbed by work on the ski pistes but in general
the path is easy to follow.

From Stafal take the trail which heads up north with great views of the Lys glacier, then east into the Salza Valley. At the head of this valley is the **Colle della Salza** (2890m) reached in about 2hrs 30mins. A 30mins descent leads to the **Orestes Hütte**.

The **Orestes Hütte** (2600m) is relatively new and doesn't appear on the maps at the time of writing. The hut is a proud emblem of the Walser culture, dedicated to the memory of Oreste Squinobal (1942–2004), a renowned alpinist of Walser origin. It offers fine regional food and small rooms for a night of comfort, albeit at a slightly higher price. The next day the TMR route over the Col d'Olen is easily reached in just over an hour (see Stage 4).

STAGE 4
Gabiet to Alagna/Pastore

Start	Gabiet (2342m); or the Orestes Hütte (2600m)
Finish	Alagna (1180m); or Rifugio Pastore (1575m)
Distance	11.5km; 15.5km to Rifugio Pastore
Total ascent	546m; 941m to Rifugio Pastore
Total descent	1748m
Time	4½hrs; 6hrs to Rifugio Pastore
High point	Col d'Olen (2881m)
Maps	1:50,000 IGC 5 Cervino-Matterhorn e Monte Rosa; 1:25,000 IGC 109 Monte Rosa Alagna Macugnaga Gressoney
Transport	You could take the cable car up to Passo dei Salati and walk round and down to pick up the TMR trail near the Col d'Olen. You could also take lifts to reach Alagna, either all the way from the Passo dei Salati or from the middle station at Alpe Pianalunga. A bus – July and August only – goes from Alagna to the Acqua Bianca waterfall, from where it's just 20mins walk to Rifugio Pastore.

Access	To start: By ski lifts and on foot. To finish: Alagna is reached by road from Novara, in the main valley near Milan. A road continues onwards some way towards Rifugio Pastore, but the final part must be done on foot.
Accommodation	Rifugio Città di Mortara, Rifugio d'Otro (also known as Zar Senni); Alagna hotels; Rifugio Pastore
Notes	Some maps show the Gressoney cable car going up to the Col d'Olen. This is not correct; it goes a little higher, to Passo dei Salati. If you take any lifts, or if you take the variant via Vallico di Cimalegno along the Vallone delle Pisse, this will seem to be a short stage, but do not be tempted to try to go on beyond Rifugio Pastore. There are no more accommodation options before the end of Stage 5, which is a full day's walk.
Variant	A route direct to the Rifugio Pastore along the Vallone delle Pisse gives exciting and remote walking, but only in good weather and when there is no névé on the slopes. It is not always open because of the risk of rockfall in the base of the valley.
Facilities	If you go above Col d'Olen to the Passo dei Salati there is a bar restaurant open during the cable car season. Rifugio Pastore sells snacks (chocolate and biscuits) and has a lunchtime meal service. Picnics for the next day are provided if you order the evening before. Alagna has all necessary facilities.
Escape route	From Alagna it is a very long way to get to anywhere else on the trek. A bail-out here would involve driving down to Novara then up to Aosta.

The initial walk up from Gabiet is neither scenic nor easy but once at the Col d'Olen you enter a different world. Gone are the tracks and cables and lifts. Here is a wild world of brooding dark rock faces, plunging valleys, far-off misty mountain ranges and, if you're lucky, herds of ibex grazing the bouldery slopes.

You could walk down to the lift station at Alpe Pianalunga and take a cable car to Alagna or follow a poorly maintained path from there, but the

Tour takes a fabulous route down to the Devil's Rock then across to the Passo Foric which leads into the Valle d'Otro, renowned for its traditional Walser hamlets. The Rifugio Zar Senni in the hamlet of Otro offers a most tempting place to stop for the night – passing by on a sunny afternoon even the most hardened hiker will find it difficult to resist the idea of setting down his heavy pack and lounging on the grazed grassy slopes in the heat. An easy but quite long trail continues down from Otro through forest to emerge at Alagna.

From the Orestes Hütte a clear trail leads south to join the TMR about half way up the ascent from Gabiet to the Col d'Olen.

◀ The trail up from Gabiet, initially a reasonable footpath, soon meets the ski pistes heading northeast. Underfoot is not pretty – the usual mess of ski areas – but look up and enjoy the ever-improving views of snowy summits. Liskamm dominates, along with the sub-summits of Monte Rosa.

Keep a look out for the yellow **TMR waymarks** for this section but don't worry too much if you lose them as they can get obscured by work on the pistes. If you lose sight of the paint flashes follow the wide tracks.

Walking this section proves that the optimal slope gradient for skiers is not the same as for walkers – whether ascending or descending, these tracks do not seem very kind on the legs. However, this ascent is fairly short-lived

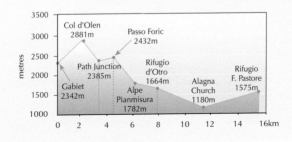

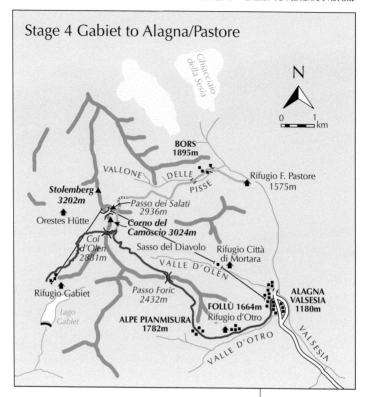

Stage 4 Gabiet to Alagna/Pastore

and not far from the Col d'Olen a rather nasty-looking slope takes you to a path going to the col. ▶

The ski area is quickly forgotten as the joys of this high, barren col are discovered.

The Monte Rosa massif rears up from the plains and forms the extreme southern edge of the Pennine Alps. Warm air coming up from Lake Maggiore encounters this huge obstacle and is forced to rise up over it, cooling rapidly in the process and thus forming water vapour. For this reason the **Col**

You'll quite probably be greeted by ibex grazing the slopes and there may be big males right on the trail. They are not usually too spooked by hikers as long as you stay calm.

103

Looking across to the next day's stage during the descent from the Col d'Olen

d'Olen is a notoriously foggy spot, but hopefully you will be there in clear sunshine and will be able to appreciate the extensive views dropping away down to the Valsesia and way beyond down the Po Valley. In addition to the Rifugio Città di Vigevano (currently closed), there is also a huge building just to the north which looks like a 5-star hotel but is in fact a scientific research centre.

Although the Col d'Olen is in the midst of the Gressoney and Alagna ski areas, the surrounding landscape, especially on the Alagna side, is a hiker's paradise. If you have extra time the small peak of Corno del Camoscio 3024m provides an exciting detour up on the left and if you look carefully you might find the intense dark blue King of the Alps flowers nestling among the summit rocks.

From the Col d'Olen take the path which descends south-east down the slopes below. Soon a junction is reached with a path descending from the Rifugio Città di Vigevano.

The big boulder here is the Sasso del Diavolo, the **Devil's Rock**, and is split into two pieces. The name comes from legend: the story goes that the Devil wanted to destroy the church at Gressoney. He brought a big rock up from Gabiet to the small peak of Corno del Camoscio, and from the top he dropped the rock down, intending it to roll down onto Gressoney, but it went down the other side. Understandably annoyed, the Devil walked down to the rock and split it with a well-aimed head butt.

Continue on path number 5. Below, the lift station at Alpe Pianalunga is obvious, as are the ski pistes leading to it. However, these are soon left behind. At a second junction a trail heads away from the ski area, across the hillside in a rising traverse to the **Passo Foric** (2432m), on the ridge which descends from Corno Rosso. The junction trail sign gives 20mins to the pass which seems a touch optimistic, but it's not much of a climb. From the

Walser buildings at Otro

pass the views are wonderful back to the Col d'Olen and the mighty glaciated Liskamm behind.

Now the terrain is grassy and wild, the ski resort a distant memory. At first the trail is indistinct, but head straight down (southeast) and you'll soon pick it up. The path is narrow and does not seem like a major route. It stays on the left of the Otro Valley, winding down through bushes and flowers. ◀ High cliffs dominate the far side of the cwm.

This trail is quite narrow and bushy – in wet weather it can be a bit unpleasant!

After some time the first house appears on a promontory on the right – the nicely restored hamlet of **Alpe Pianmisura** (1782m). Other dwellings follow and the trail gets wider. There are several examples of Walser architecture here: look out for the wooden frames for drying hay on the sunny sides of the chalets.

The bushes give way to grassy Alpine meadows and the oasis of **Otro** is reached, a well-known Walser settlement with an attractive church.

This beautiful **summer Alp** can only be described as paradise, especially on a lovely day in the warmth of the afternoon sun. The Rifugio d'Otro (Rifugio Zar Senni) is right by the footpath and a night spent here would be memorable.

A wide track leads on into the woods. You may feel that the descent is nearly over but you would be mistaken; the way down through the forest is quite long, although the trail is good. Oratories are placed strategically by the wayside, evidence that this path has served for centuries as the route to the summer farms.

At a junction go left past a farm to emerge on a small road where a right turn will take you to the village of **Alagna**. ◀

If you have come down by cable car you will be dropped just behind the church in the centre of Alagna.

Alagna has its own particular charms. In addition to the more obvious delights of village life – bars, pastry shops, attractive wooden chalets – there is also the Walser Museum which deserves a visit if you decide to stay in town. This is the highest village

in the Valsesia, which runs down towards Milan and the main Po Valley. The church is beautifully decorated in traditional style, and there are many wooden Walser chalets to admire. Even if you are going on up to Rifugio Pastore, take time to explore.

The Otro Valley is a pastoral paradise for walkers

Extension to Rifugio Pastore
To get to **Pastore** follow the road out of the village, north, past the feldspar mine. After about 3km the road goes over the river but a trail goes straight on and leads up to the hut.

> **Rifugio Pastore** is a very convenient and convivial place to stay as it leaves you poised for the following day's long ascent to the Colle del Turlo. In good weather there are the most wonderful views of the mighty Southeast Face of Monte Rosa, and in the evening you'll be able to spot the lights of the Rifugio Regina Margherita perched 2000m above on the summit of the Signalkuppe. This is the highest hut in Europe at 4559m. Built in 1893 and

Dawn light on the Monte Rosa peaks as seen from Rifugio Pastore

VARIANT DIRECT TO RIFUGIO PASTORE

Another option from the Col d'Olen is a shorter, more direct route over the col marked Vallico di Cimalegno. **This route is poorly waymarked and vague in places and not recommended for inexperienced trekkers or in bad visibility.** A head for heights in needed for this descent.

The route heads northeast along a vague ridge for about 500m. This path is marked 5e on the 1:25,000 map, but you need to keep your eyes open to see the waymarks as the route goes over rocky boulders. At the col marked Vallico di Cimalegno find the trail that goes down northeast into the cwm above the aptly named Vallone delle Pisse – the massive vertical waterfall that plunges directly down cliffs at the head of the lower valley was presumably the inspiration for the name.

This trail is waymarked 10b but is quite unfrequented. It goes down shaly slopes through rocks, sometimes a little airy with one tiny downclimb, to come out on scree slopes underneath the big Indren cable car, becoming quite vague as it reaches the meadows. Go beyond the lake (north) and, at a ruin, pick up path 10c which zigzags down to a lower cwm where there is an ugly concrete disused cable car station at La Balma. From La Balma the trail is clearly defined as it traverses under the impressive Cascata delle Pisse, to the pleasant valley and the old buildings of **Alpe Bors**.

An old mule track descends the steep slope down to the meadows of Alpe Blatte. Be sure to take a break here and look left – Monte Rosa can be seen in all its glory. Then head on down Alpe Pile to **Rifugio Pastore**.

TRANSHUMANCE

Young goatherd taking his charges up to the higher meadows

Transhumance describes the tradition whereby farmers move their cattle around according to seasonal changes, in search of optimum grazing conditions. In the Alps the farmer lives in a valley village in winter and keeps his cattle indoors in a barn. He does very little farming during the harsh cold months, just providing hay every day for his animals (in some regions of Switzerland a law decrees that cattle must be put outside at some stage every day throughout the year). As spring arrives the cattle are put out to graze the fresh grass in the lower meadows next to the village. As the weather warms up gradually the grass grows at higher altitudes. The farmer's first move will be to higher meadows not too far above the village. He will own a small farm there where he stays for several weeks while his animals graze; he milks them, and will often make cheese.

Once the summer is well established the farmer will take his cattle up to a higher farm above the treeline, often around the 2000m mark. Here they will spend the rest of the summer, and the farmer will take his family to live up there too. Cheese will be produced for the winter, as well as other dairy products. They may also grow crops in the surrounding meadows, and in the past would certainly have grown enough for their own summer needs.

When the days begin to get shorter and colder it's time to head down to the village again. This is often a celebration in the Alps; a successful summer season means there will be enough food to keep everyone supplied over the coming winter. The cattle may be adorned with flowers, and the whole village comes out to see their return. A few weeks are spent grazing the valley fields before once again the animals are quartered inside.

Transhumance is still practised throughout the Alps. When walking you will often come across these summer farms, and sometimes find cheese and milk for sale. Some also provide basic hut accommodation for walkers, and are often great places to stay where the evening meal will be a truly traditional affair.

renovated in 1980 the hut gives shelter every year to climbers and scientists from all over the world.

If you arrive early at Rifugio Pastore then enjoy a beer on their fine terrace, or study the orientation table which details all the facets of Monte Rosa to be seen from this wonderful vantage point; There is also an interesting botanical garden just a few minutes up the hill.

Beware, however, that because of its accessibility from the road, and the fact that it's a great hut, Rifugio Pastore is popular and often full. Don't turn up without a reservation.

STAGE 5
Alagna/Pastore to Macugnaga

Start	Alagna (1180m); or Rifugio Pastore (1575m)
Finish	Macugnaga (Staffa) (1317m)
Distance	20km; or 16km from Rifugio Pastore
Total ascent	1649m; or 1254m from Rifugio Pastore
Total descent	1512m
Time	9–10hrs; or 8+hrs from Rifugio Pastore
High point	Colle del Turlo (2738m)
Maps	1:50,000 IGC 5 Cervino-Matterhorn e Monte Rosa; 1:25,000 IGC 109 Monte Rosa Alagna Macugnaga Gressoney
Transport	None until you reach Macugnaga, where a two-part cable car goes up almost to the Monte Moro Pass
Access	To start: Alagna is reached by road from Novara, in the main valley near Milan. A road continues some way towards Rifugio Pastore, but the final part must be done on foot. To finish: By road from Domodossola, which can be reached from Switzerland via Brig or from Italy via Novara or Milan.
Accommodation	Alagna hotels; Macugnaga hotels; Rifugio Pastore

Variant	This is the easiest way to walk from the Valsesia to the Valle Anzasca. There is no alternative (other than a very long bus ride).
Facilities	Alagna has all necessary facilities; Rifugio Pastore sells basic snacks (biscuits and chocolate) and will provide a picnic if you order the evening before; Macugnaga has several grocery shops as well as a newsagents and several cafés.
Conditions	The trail is good, and bad weather – other than storms or snow – should not be a problem. Névé quite often remains near the col, on the north side, and if this is frozen it could be very icy, although by the time the descent is reached any snow slopes should have softened unless the temperatures are very cold.
Escape route	Turn around!

This day features the somewhat formidable Colle del Turlo. But in essence the route is simple – one ascent and one descent. The col has seen traffic since medieval times as it is the only direct way from the Valsesia to the Macugnaga Valley. It's a good honest mountain day, and if you take your eyes off the trail and look around there's plenty to see. The path is excellent.

From Rifugio Pastore the route takes a beautifully maintained mule track up to the higher meadows, and this good path continues all the way up to the pass. But it's the far side that sees the mother of all trail maintenance: you won't see better than this in Europe! Huge rock slabs guide you down this most aesthetic winding stairway, past the red Lanti bivouac hut and its neighbour (a godsend in bad weather), along a wide ledge bisected at intervals by gushing streams, then into the alder bushes which clear to reveal the summer alpage at La Piana, with its cross. A more standard trail continues on through forest, down the Valle Quarazza, eventually to emerge at Quarazza itself where there is a welcome café next to a lake. There follows an easy track alongside the Anza Torrent and up into Macugnaga.

To get to **Pastore** follow the road out of Alagna, north, past the feldspar mine. After about 3km the road goes over the river but a trail goes straight on and leads up to the hut.

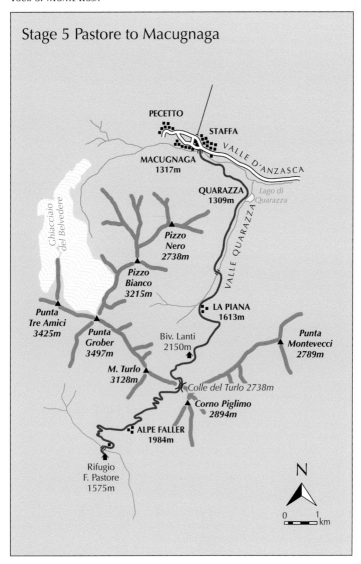

Stage 5 Pastore to Macugnaga

PECETTO

STAFFA

VALLE D'ANZASCA

MACUGNAGA
1317m

QUARAZZA
1309m

Lago di
Quarazza

Chiacciaio
del Belvedere

Pizzo
Nero
2738m

VALLE QUARAZZA

Pizzo
Bianco
3215m

LA PIANA
1613m

Punta
Tre Amici
3425m

Punta
Grober
3497m

Biv. Lanti
2150m

Punta
Montevecci
2789m

M. Turlo
3128m

Colle del Turlo 2738m

Corno Piglimo
2894m

ALPE FALLER
1984m

Rifugio
F. Pastore
1575m

N

0   1
▭▭▭▭▭ km

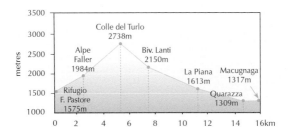

A good track sets off from Rifugio Pastore and crosses the river by a covered bridge to Alpe Blatte where the old farm buildings have been renovated. The trail quickly enters forest and a good mule track leads up to the higher summer grazing meadows at **Alpe Faller** (1984m).

Take advantage of the **wonderful views** not only of Monte Rosa but also the route of Stage 4 behind you; the panorama gives ample excuse to stop and catch your breath.

Unusually the Colle del Turlo is provided with table and chairs

The well-made path takes a fairly gentle gradient, following near to the Acqua Bianca stream, source of the impressive waterfall below. At around 2300m it steepens to ascend to the **Colle del Turlo** (2738m) in a series of long zigzags.

> The pass is a sort of **brèche**, a narrow saddle surrounded by rocks, with a metal plaque that celebrates the Italian alpini troops. You can set out your picnic on a huge rock slab table that looks like it belongs in Fred Flintstone's house, complete with a set of matching benches.
>
> Here you leave the Valsesia, so enjoy the views on the south side before stepping through to a new vista. Ahead to the north are the impressive mountains forming the frontier with Switzerland, while far below are the Quarazza and Anzasca valleys.

Old snow patches on the start of the descent from the Colle del Turlo

Now take the paved trail, which you'd be hard pushed to lose unless it's hidden by snow. Sometimes these initial northern slopes hold névé well into the summer, in which case great care must be taken as the ground could be very slippery.

IBEX

Ibex near the Col d'Olen

There are several places on the Tour of Monte Rosa where you may catch a glimpse of an ibex. This mountain goat can often be found grazing peacefully on the higher rocky slopes, especially early and late in the day.

Ibex can be recognised by their characteristic ridged horns, which grow to a considerable length in older males. This animal has always provoked admiration for its fine profile, as well as its sturdy build and ability to survive in the most hostile of environments. Sadly for many centuries ibex were not only hunted as food but also for trophy (horns). The species was almost extinct 150 years ago, and only survived thanks to the actions of the Italian King Victor Emmanuel who created a hunting reserve in 1856, now the Gran Paradiso National Park. Ibex from the park have been reintroduced throughout the Alps, where they are now totally protected.

Male ibex can weigh more than 100kg; their horns can reach 90cm long and weigh up to 5kg. Males fight for dominance of the herd by rearing up on their hind legs and clashing horns. Such displays are to be seen in late summer and early autumn. Their hooves are especially adapted for rocky terrain, having an elastic sole, which makes them less agile on snow than the chamois. It is not rare to encounter an ibex making its way, quite at ease, up or down steep rock slabs only really suitable for rock climbing.

The ibex fur is beige brown, becoming darker with age, and the winter coat is a deeper brown. In spring they lose this thick coat, which often hangs in clumps off their backs. Ibex will usually not live much beyond 15 years, and the old males tend to spend their final years in relative isolation. It is not unusual to see single ibex, but females and young tend to stay in groups.

Although relatively undisturbed by human presence the ibex will emit a sharp whistle of alarm if they feel threatened, and will sometimes find a place from where they can kick stones down onto you. They have few natural predators, although the golden eagle will take young and can sometimes use a nifty wing manoeuvre to unbalance larger animals, causing them to fall off cliffs.

The hamlet shown on the 1:25,000 map at Alpe Schena (1987m) is in ruins.

Soon the trail passes near the **Bivouac Lanti** (2150m), where there are two buildings, both of which are usually open and provide useful shelter for lunch in case of rain. A long contour provides easy walking, and water sources from the streams that flow over the trail, before the route descends once more in an area of alder bushes. ◄

On the map this part of the descent looks really steep, but the many zigzags make it relatively painless and soon the flat area of **La Piana** (1613m) is reached. The cross and the surrounding flat rocks provide an obvious place for a break and the opportunity to savour this fabulous cwm, dominated by the high peaks of Punta Grober and Pizzo Bianco. The slopes round about are favoured by chamois, so keep your eyes open for grazing herds.

From La Piana the trail reverts to an old mule track used to access the high summer farms and wanders through forest, near the river, and past an abandoned iron mine at 1360m, with a renovated Italian Alpine Club hut that is now private. Not long now before you can take a break at the welcome café at **Quarazza** – sit outside with a cold drink and watch the fishermen by the lake before girding your loins for the final part of the walk.

A wide track/road goes around past Isella, following the Anza river, which on a hot afternoon is a raging torrent of meltwater coming down directly from the glaciers of Monte Rosa. After a couple of kilometres you'll arrive in **Macugnaga** and can relax before an evening stroll around the village.

Macugnaga is another interesting Alpine town, situated in the back of beyond and almost forgotten, snugly shoehorned into this corner of Italy nestled up against the Swiss border.

Little known it may be, but it can be incredibly difficult to pre-book a hotel room in mid-season for one night. This is one reason you may consider continuing up to the Rifugio Oberto Maroli (Stage 6) just below the Monte Moro Pass. All but the most masochistic of hikers will probably have had their fill of walking when they reach Macugnaga, so you will be more or less obliged to take the cable car. ▶

Check the time of the last ascent before you plan this stage.

STAGE 6
Macugnaga to Saas Fee

Start	Macugnaga (Staffa) (1317m)
Finish	Saas Fee (1803m)
Distance	20km
Total ascent	1536m
Total descent	1180m
Time	11hrs (2 days)
High point	Monte Moro Pass (2853m)
Maps	1:50,000 Carte Nationale de la Suisse 5006 Matterhorn Mischabel; 1:25,000 IGC 109 Monte Rosa Alagna Macugnaga Gressoney; Carte Nationale de la Suisse 1349 Monte Moro; 1329 Saas
Transport	The cable car goes from Macugnaga in two sections to just below Monte Moro Pass; from Mattmark there is a bus to Saas Almagell, from where another bus goes to Saas Fee.
Access	To start: By road from Domodossala, which can be reached from Switzerland via Brig or from Italy via Novara or Milan. To finish: Saas Fee is accessed by road up the Saastal, which coincides with the Mattertal at Stalden. There is road and train access to Stalden from Visp and Brig in the Rhône Valley.
Accommodation	Macugnaga hotels; Rifugio Oberto Maroli (Rifugio Oberto Gaspare or Rifugio Città di Malnate on some maps); Saas Almagell, Saas Grund and Saas Fee hotels
Note	This is not a one-day stage if you walk it all. You need to stay at the Rifugio Oberto Maroli to then have plenty of time to do the long stretch down from Monte Moro and all the way down the Saas Valley to Saas Almagell and up to Saas Fee. If you do not stay at the hut you need to select one or more of the transport options.
Variant	No suitable variant for this stage.

Facilities	Macugnaga, Saas Almagell, Saas Grund and Saas Fee have all kinds of facilities. Snacks and drinks available at the Rifugio Oberto Maroli, if open. Café at Mattmark.
Conditions	Early in the season névé often lingers on the slopes of Monte Moro, which can make passage difficult. The southern slopes are less likely to be snowy in the summer; if they are, the lift (if running) can be taken. However, the northern slopes down to Mattmark do hold snow and the section with cables along rock slabs can become delicate.
Escape route	Once en route the aim is to get over the border into Switzerland. The only way around is to return to Macugnaga and take the bus to Domodossola, then the train to Brig and Stalden with a bus at the end to Saas Fee.

The high point, in all senses, of this long stage is the Monte Moro Pass at 2853m and the nearby summit at 2984m. This col is situated right under the East Face of Monte Rosa and is somewhere you may well wish to linger in good weather. The pass forms the access route back to Switzerland and the excellent Rifugio Oberto Maroli is just below on the Italian side. The views more than compensate for the rather ugly ski resort paraphernalia.

The Swiss side of Monte Moro is nothing short of magical. Rocky slabs (equipped for a very short section with cables) give way to grassy meadows, interspersed with gently babbling brooks which take you down to the lake at Mattmark. A pleasant track gives some rare flat walking, allowing you to enjoy the views of the Saas peaks, such as the Strahlhorn.

There is nowhere to stay at Mattmark so you must either walk on down to the Saas Valley and stay somewhere there or take the bus, changing at Saas Almagell, to reach Saas Fee. The trail down from Mattmark to Saas Almagell is not the most interesting part of the TMR but it is restful after all those high passes and then you finish with a gentle climb through forest up to Saas Fee.

Head out of town past the church and the lift station. A good trail is signed on the right which winds up through

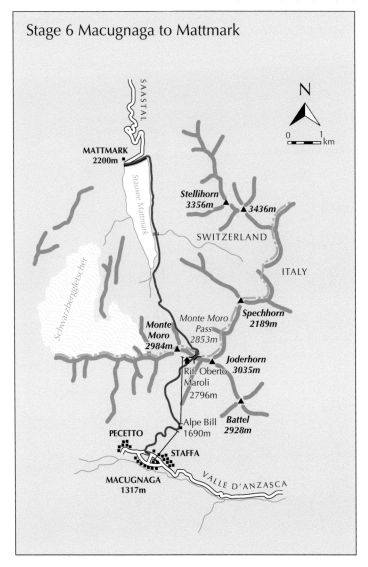

Stage 6 Macugnaga to Mattmark

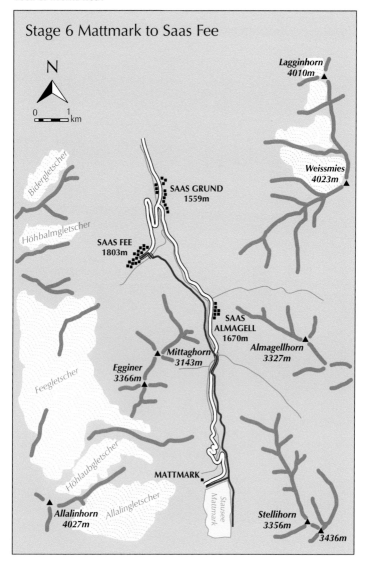

Stage 6 Mattmark to Saas Fee

N

0 — 1 km

Bidergletscher

Höhbalmgletscher

Lagginhorn
4010m ▲

Weissmies
4023m ▲

SAAS GRUND
1559m

SAAS FEE
1803m

Feegletscher

**SAAS
ALMAGELL**
1670m

Almagellhorn
3327m

▲ *Mittaghorn*
3143m

Egginer
3366m ▲

Höhlaubgletscher

MATTMARK

*Stausee
Mattmark*

▲ *Allalinhorn*
4027m

Allalingletscher

Stellihorn
3356m ▲

▲ *3436m*

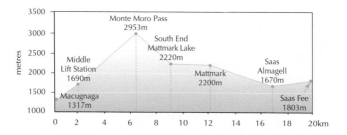

forest. ▶ It heads right at the treeline across to the mid station at the top of the first cable car at 1690m (Alpe Bill).

The path onwards is less defined, but is generally signed in red and white flashes and sometimes yellow TMR waymarks. It climbs directly uphill (northeast) through bushes and past streams; in rain this section can get quite marshy. A bigger trail is joined which comes across from Alpe Sonnobierg at about 2000m. This winds around under the cable car until it reaches a smaller lift. The trail more or less follows this lift, then another higher up, and is waymarked in red and white. In good visibility this is easy to follow, but in fog or when there is névé on the ground it is really easy to lose the path on these higher slopes. If in doubt keep in sight of the high lift cables.

Near the top the path goes up rocks until a traverse left to the **Rifugio Oberto Maroli** (2796m), situated to the right (east) of the cable car station.

The **Oberto Maroli refuge** offers a full lunch menu in an attractive dining room, and an annexe has been renovated to provide several small dormitories with very good facilities. In the morning the high

This is an ancient access route for the summer farms so it's well-worn from centuries of feet and hooves.

121

The Macugnaga Valley seen from the slopes of Monte Moro

soaring walls of Monte Rosa's East Face turn pink in the rays of the rising sun and if you decide to stay the night at the hut it would be easy to include an ascent of the nearby Joderhorn (3035m).

There are paintmarks all around the lift and hut area; continue over to the station then follow more waymarks which go northeast and soon lead to easy-angled rock slabs equipped with chains. These are used to climb up to a rather grand shining golden statue of the Madonna a few metres above the Monte Moro Pass. This is a very popular spot – many holidaymakers take the lift up from Macugnaga – and you can see why.

If the weather is good, the views are stupendous in all directions: west is Monte Rosa, northeast the Saastal, with the peaks of the Weissmies and the Lagginhorn on the east side of the valley. However, fog is not unknown here, so don't be surprised if you're on the Monte Moro Pass and can't see your hand in front of your face. The **Madonna della Nevi** (Madonna of the Snow) is also the objective of religious pilgrimages on Catholic Feast Days, notably 4/5 August when there will almost certainly be a long procession of people making their way up to Monte Moro from the Italian and Swiss sides of the mountain.

The golden Madonna guarding the Monte Moro Pass

LARCH

Larch trees in their autumn glory

The larch (*Larix decidua*) is essentially a mountain tree. It flourishes in the Alps up to an altitude of 2000m and more and is found in the Apennines and Carpathians, but is unknown in its wild state in the Pyrenees, or in the Spanish or Scandinavian peninsulas.

It grows best on sloping mountainsides, where its roots can spread out deep into the ground. The trunk is tapering, covered in scaly reddish-grey bark and shaggy tufts of hoary lichen. Larch is regarded as the best wood for building houses in the mountains, as it needs no protective treatment and ages quite naturally. The oldest chalets seen on Alpine treks will be built of larch, and the façade that faces away from the prevailing weather will be a deep reddish colour.

In favourable conditions the larch grows to a height upwards of 30m and its trunk can attain 1m diameter or more. It is the only conifer to have deciduous foliage and it loses its needles after a fine display of autumn colours, to grow new soft green tufts in the spring. It has male and female flowers, the latter being a delightful deep pink. The flowers then form small cones.

The larch is known for its resin, known as Venice Turpentine, which is collected in certain regions by tapping into the sap of healthy trees. This turpentine takes the name of Venice after being shipped from that port. Venice has derived not only turpentine from the larch but also the piles on which the city is built – a strong testimony to its durability under the most destructive conditions. The swathes of larch forest found in the Alps provide a splendid contrast to the usual dark pine and spruce, and the variety of colour gives a welcome reminder of the seasons. However, not everyone agrees. Wordsworth, for example, wrote of the larch: 'Its branches have no variety and little dignity…in summer it is of a dingy lifeless hue, in autumn of a spiritless, unvaried yellow and in winter the larch appears absolutely dead.' But what did he know?

Waymarks lead you down through rocks to the **Monte Moro Pass** (2853m). Say 'Arriverderci' to Italy and step into Switzerland.

On the trail from Monte Moro Pass to Mattmark

The trail is rocky for the first part, taking in a variety of slabs and ledges, interspersed with easier ground. The route is never difficult, except in snow, but for comfort and fast progress it does require a reasonably stable footing in places. The Tälli cwm is most impressive, formed by high rocky peaks, scree slopes and several deep streams. Once past the rocky section the path becomes a lot gentler and soon you arrive at a flat area where there is a big boulder with path signs painted on it; a good place for a rest and to enjoy this wonderful Alpine cirque.

Another trail comes in from the right here and both paths join to descend grassy slopes strewn with boulders to **Mattmark Lake**. ▶

Look back to Monte Moro – those with keen eyesight will be able to discern the gleaming Madonna proudly atop her col.

The lake is a popular objective for holidaymakers who can drive up to the dam at the northern end and then walk along its shores. There is a road on the west side, although car access seems to be limited. The trail along the east shore is better for walking, and is bordered with many interesting Alpine flowers. This is a welcome

125

On the descent to Mattmark Lake

section of flat hiking, not often encountered on an Alpine trek. The Saas peaks are in view, notably the Strahlhorn, with their glaciers tumbling down towards the Saas Valley far below.

At the end of the lake, cross the dam if you want to have a drink at the Mattmark café just below the dam before setting off down into the valley. The bus goes from the car park here. Otherwise continue straight on: the trail is waymarked in red and white and flirts with the road for much of the way. It is 11km from here to Saas Fee. ◀ The path stays on the right of the road, which is next to the river, all the way to Saas Almagell, with the final section actually on the road.

Don't underestimate this stretch – lower in altitude it may be, but covering such a distance takes time, and finishing in the dark is not always a desirable end to the day.

If you are going on to Saas Grund there is a valley route on the left of the river from Saas Almagell. Otherwise, to go on up to **Saas Fee**, pick up the trail that heads left and into the forest. This track contours around the hillside gently gaining height until it arrives in Saas Fee at Zum Steg. Cross the river and head into town.

STAGE 7
Saas Fee to Grächen

Start	Saas Fee (1803m)
Finish	Grächen (1619m)
Distance	16km
Total ascent	About 700m
Total descent	About 900m
Time	8hrs
High point	Stock (2360m)
Maps	1:50,000 Carte Nationale de la Suisse 5006 Matterhorn Mischabel; 1:25,000 Carte Nationale de la Suisse 1329 Saas; 1328 Randa; 1308 St Niklaus
Transport	Cable car down from Hannigalp to Grächen
Access	To start: Saas Fee is accessed by road up the Saastal, which meets the Mattertal at Stalden. To reach Stalden there is road and train access from Visp and Brig in the Rhône Valley. To finish: Grächen is reached from the Mattertal by bus from St Niklaus.
Accommodation	Saas Fee hotels; Grächen hotels
Variant	No options for this stage.
Warning	Although this trail is very popular with locals and visitors alike, it is not to be underestimated. Some sections involve arduous walking over boulders, and there are long stages of exposed path which some people will find unsettling.
Facilities	Saas Fee and Grächen are both small tourist towns with all necessary facilities. No cafés along the route until you reach Hannigalp.
Conditions	The Höhenweg is a much-used trail but can still be prone to landslides and rockfall in bad weather. Equally, animals can knock down stones from above. Take your breaks in open areas away from the slopes.
Escape route	Various paths lead off the Höhenweg down into the Saastal from where the bus can be used to return to the start point; notably down to Ze Briggiltinu about halfway along the trail.

The Saastal is divided from the Mattertal by the lofty Mischabel peaks, extending from the Strahlhorn to Balfrin. All passes through this range are glaciated, but luckily the walker can pass from one valley to the next along a high balcony path known as the Höhenweg (high way). One of the pleasantest trails on the Tour of Monte Rosa, this balcony footpath leads from Saas Fee to Grächen, traversing along the eastern slopes of Balfrin.

As with all balcony paths the views can only be described as stunning – the only quibble might be that some of the most spectacular peaks are behind you as you progress along the trail. This time it's the Saastal peaks with which you become familiar, notably the Weissmies, Lagginhorn and Fletschhorn.

At the end of the day the path turns the Grossi Furgge ridge at Hannigalp, and you're greeted by a new panorama: the Mattertal peaks, dominated by the Weisshorn, a summit you'll have plenty of time to admire during Stage 8.

The **Höhenweg Grächen** (opened in 1954) soon rises up from Saas Fee and then stays around the 2100–2200m level. Old farming trails have been used, enhanced by a certain amount of blasting and tunnelling to allow access across rocky walls. The terrain is varied, ranging from forest track to open trail bordered with bilberry bushes and juniper, to rocky boulders and short sections of exposed ledge. Animals are often seen grazing the steep slopes below, seemingly unperturbed by the passage of walkers.

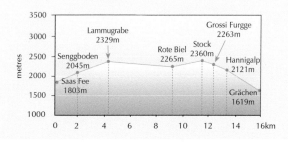

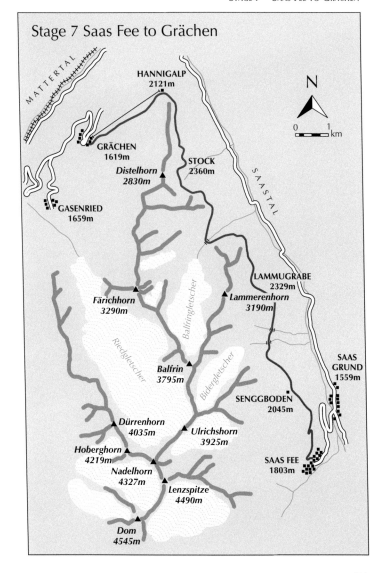

Stage 7 Saas Fee to Grächen

Typical terrain on the Höhenweg – wonderful walking but little space to stop and rest

The trail is justifiably popular in both directions. In general it is a much more stable route than the Europaweg (Stage 8), but there have been problems near to Saas Fee and for a few years it was rerouted along a lower level. There is now at least one metal tunnel to protect the trail from rockfall, but this has been damaged already, requiring further maintenance. ▸

In the case of problems along the Höhenweg an alternative way will be signposted.

The route is signposted from the tourist office in the centre of Saas Fee. Make your way to the northern end of town, Wildi, to enter the woods. At the first clearing bear left to a footpath junction up and left.

This is Bärefalle (1753m). Signs lead uphill and other paths join from the left. Just keep following signs for Grächen until you emerge from the trees onto higher slopes strewn with alpenrose. At Senggboden (2045m) a path comes up from Sengg. After crossing a couple of large streams you'll reach the rocky boulders above Schilti.

Legend has it that this scree slope was created by a **dragon** which was banished by the people of Saas and spent its life nibbling away at the Schilthorn, the peak above.

The trail rises up near to cliffs to reach a high point at **Lammugrabe** (2329m). There are no alternative ways here so it's a question of following your nose. After about 3hrs walking you will cross the Schweibbach stream at 2090m. There is a path down to the valley near here.

Now follows some steep climbing through boulders and forest to reach a lovely vantage point, with a seat, at Rote Biel (2265m). Stop here for a break to enjoy the views across the valley and of the Balfrin Glacier above. If the seat is occupied then just beyond is a good flat area of rock. ▸

On such trails there are few places to sit down as in general the route traverses steep slopes (definitely so from here on).

Open slopes allow views all the way down towards Visp, but most of the time you'll be keeping your eyes on the path as it is quite exposed in places. Traverse the

Grossus Gufer cwm and then continue on to **Stock** where there is another bench at 2360m.

Check out those **Saastal summits** – the west-facing Weissmies Glacier is particularly prominent, and with binoculars you may be able to make out a track (the Normal Route to ascend the peak). To the north, far away in the Bernese Oberland, is the pointy summit of the Bietschorn.

The trail turns a corner and makes its way somewhat precariously through rocks, with the odd cable or handrail to help. There is a short tunnel, and a gate as the path crosses two gullies. These slopes can erode in bad weather so do take care.

Undulating ground follows, mainly downhill as the trail heads round under the Grossi Furgge ridge, but not without the odd 'up' to catch you out. Finally a junction is reached; both paths go to Hannigalp and the lower one

Runners on the Höhenweg

MARMOTS

Marmots enjoy the sun; during the summer months they have to feed up so as to survive the long winter hibernation

The marmot is perhaps the animal that most characterises the Alps. Before the Ice Age marmots were found throughout central and western Europe, but after the glaciers retreated 10,000 years ago the lower regions became covered in forest, unsuitable habitat for marmots, so these small furry creatures headed up to the mountains where conditions suit them perfectly.

Marmots are about the size of a fat cat, sturdy in build with short legs, wide paws, claws and a short round head. Their fur varies in colour from grey to beige or even a reddish hue. They prefer areas that are clear of vegetation so that they can spot predators, and are found mainly in meadows, bouldery areas and scree slopes, and at the edges of sparse larch forest.

Marmots are very social creatures and live in groups. They are on constant lookout for danger, and their high-pitched whistles will often accompany you during your Alpine hikes. Look around and you'll likely spot one perched high on a rock, standing on his hind legs, giving the danger sign to his fellows. At this sound they all scurry down their burrows, only to pop out again minutes later. No longer hunted by man, their principle predators are eagles and foxes. Marmots spend the summer months eating and getting ready for autumn when they hibernate in their burrows for six months or more. It is said that the young marmots have the job of waking every so often and walking around the burrow to heat it up and so prevent the temperature dropping too low. The animals come out of their burrows in spring thin and weakened –a dangerous time for them until they get their energy reserves up. They reproduce in early spring and the young are born after about five weeks. During the summer the babies are often to be seen playing near the burrows under the watchful eye of an adult.

Huge old church bells in Grächen

is the flattest, coming around the ridge to the chapel at **Hannigalp** (2121m), which is quite a modern affair.

Here at the top of the cable car there are **picnic tables**, farm buildings and a great view of the Weisshorn, that superb sculpted mountain that you will come to know and love during the next stage on the Europaweg.

But for now the objective is **Grächen**. A big track goes down into the forest and descends at a fairly uncomfortable angle all the way to the road at Zumsee (1720m), a delightful hotel and restaurant with its own lake. Follow the road another 100m down to reach the main part of the attractive village of Grächen. Be sure to check out the three huge ancient bells in front of the church.

STAGE 8
Grächen to Zermatt – the Europaweg

Start	Grächen (1619m)
Finish	Zermatt (1600m)
Distance	31km
Total ascent	About 1300m
Total descent	1200m
Time	10–11hrs (2 days)
High point	Galenberg (2600m) on Europaweg
Maps	1:50,000 Carte Nationale de la Suisse 5006 Matterhorn Mischabel; 1:25,000 Carte Nationale de la Suisse 1328 Randa, 1308 St Niklaus
Transport	Sunnegga lift down to Zermatt
Access	To start: Grächen is reached by bus from the Mattertal from St Niklaus. To finish: Train from Visp; bus and road access to Täsch, then train to Zermatt.
Accommodation	Zermatt: many hotels; Täsch, Randa: hotels; Täschalp Europaweghütte; Europahütte; Gasenried: hotels; Grächen: several hotels
Note	Do not be surprised by the arduous nature of the Europaweg – although it contours around the hillside, it's best described as 'undulating'; and as usual those small ascents of 100m or so often feel a lot harder (being interspersed with descents and level sections) than a regular ascent of 1000m.
Facilities	Zermatt has everything you could ever need. You can buy chocolate at the Europahütte and if you ask the evening before they will provide a picnic. Café at Ottovan.
Escape route	There are several paths down to the valley from the Europaweg to reach Herbriggen, Randa or Täsch, from where the train can be taken to Zermatt, or the bus to Grächen or the Saas Valley.

After climbing up from Grächen to reach a statue of St Bernard on the Zum Grat ridge at around 2300m the Europaweg stays high above the

Mattertal Valley for the next 25km or so. Views of the glaciated peaks such as the Weisshorn, the Zinal Rothorn, the Obergabelhorn and, as Zermatt is reached, the Matterhorn, are unsurpassed. The Europahütte situated about halfway along the route provides a superb place to spend the night and savour these unique vistas.

There is no doubt that two days spent on the Europaweg would provide memorable walking…but only in some conditions, and these conditions are becoming increasingly rare. **It is essential to check the current state of the trail** on the Europaweg website (www.europaweg.ch) before setting out. A cautious alternative – and attractive in its own right – is to walk along the valley to Zermatt (see Stage 8A) rather than risk injury by rockfall.

A sign indicates the way out from Grächen town centre, giving 6hrs 30mins to the Europahütte and 13hrs to Zermatt. It usually takes a little less time than this, and the tourist office gives a total time of 10 or 11hrs. However long it takes this is a two-day stage, not one to go for in one long day. A small road leads past flower-bedecked chalets into forest, where a track is followed to the hamlet of **Gasenried**.

Once out of this village the Europaweg is signposted along rising forest paths, past a turn-off to the Bordierhütte.

The way is steep as most of the altitude is gained in the first couple of hours, so take it gently. From time to time **clearings** in the forest tempt you to stop for a

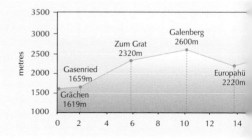

The Brunneghorn seen from Grächen

breather to enjoy glimpses of the far-off Bietschorn in the Bernese Oberland. Early on a sign on a rock identifies a source where you can fill up your water bottles. ▶

Coming out of the forest views open up and soon a grassy shoulder is reached, where a statue of St Bernard has been erected to encourage hikers on their way.

In dry conditions this is the only water fill-up point on this part of the trail.

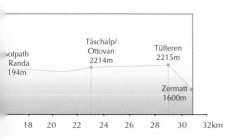

Täschalp/
Ottovan
2214m

Tüfteren
2215m

otpath
Randa
194m

Zermatt
1600m

18   20   22   24   26   28   30   32km

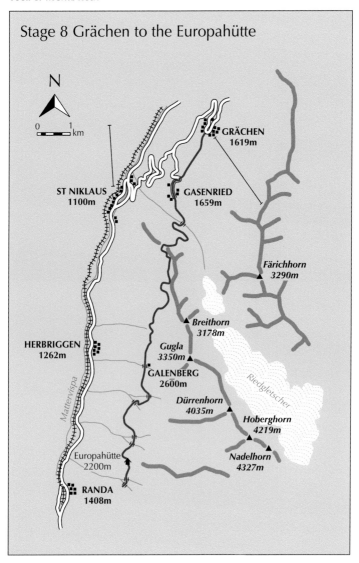

Stage 8 Grächen to the Europahütte

Stage 8 The Europahütte to Zermatt

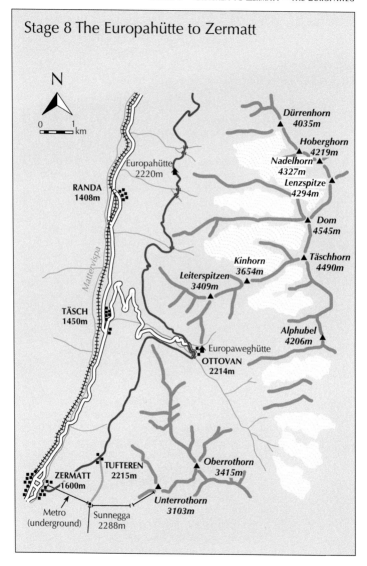

N

0   1
km

Europahütte
2220m

RANDA
1408m

▲ Dürrenhorn
4035m

Hoberghorn
4219m
Nadelhorn ●
4327m
Lenzspitze
4294m

▲ Dom
4545m

Mattervispa

Kinhorn
3654m

▲ Täschhorn
4490m

Leiterspitzen
3409m
▲

TÄSCH
1450m

Alphubel
4206m
▲

▲ Europaweghütte
OTTOVAN
2214m

ZERMATT
1600m

TUFTEREN
2215m

▲ *Oberrothorn*
3415m

▲
Unterrothorn
3103m

Metro
(underground)

Sunnegga
2288m

THE EUROPAWEG: FROM MARVEL TO MONSTER

On 6 July 1997 the Grächen Zermatt Europaweg was officially opened as a two-day hike. When first constructed it was without doubt one of the most magnificent high-terrain routes of the Alps and, along with the Saas Fee Höhenweg, was regarded as the showpiece of the Swiss Tour of Monte Rosa.

Since then things have changed somewhat and nature has taken its course. It is no longer the perfect hike it may initially seem. The Zermatt and Grächen authorities have created a monster that requires constant attention.

The trail traverses steep slopes which in winter are prone to avalanche. The high altitude of the trail ensures it is above the treeline – great for views but meaning that, inevitably, it runs across unstable ground, possibly becoming more so as a result of the melting permafrost layer deep within the earth. In heavy rain landslides are frequent and it is not uncommon for parts of the Europaweg to be closed due to risk of rockfall. This problem seems to be getting worse, despite constant trail maintenance and the construction of metal tunnels on the worst-affected slopes, enabling the walker to safely cross gullies raked by rocks. In the last few years the section of trail from the Europahütte to Täschalp has frequently been re-routed, resulting in a big descent then a big climb to get back up to the original path. At the time of writing the trail from Täschalp to Tufteren above Zermatt is closed, again due to rockfall.

Because of all this uncertainty about the state of this part of the trek conditions are likely to differ from the description given here.

Patron saint of mountaineers, **St Bernard** was active in the 11th century when he gave up a life of leisure to help the poor and needy. He saw it as his mission to help those who were obliged to travel in the mountains – for trade, immigration, pilgrimage, to find grazing and so on. He set up two hospices on mountain passes to give shelter and food to travellers and provide safe passage.

From here on the character of the trail changes totally, and for the next few hours your world will be dominated by rock and scree rather than grass and trees. The trail

This bridge near the Europahütte has had to be
replaced at least once and may no longer even exist

continues to climb, but more gently now, becoming more and more barren as it begins its long snaking traverse around the hillside. Rocky buttresses give way to steep gullies and narrow ledges. The occasional cable aids passage but you still need to keep a wary eye on the trail. Views are best enjoyed when standing still.

Galenberg (2600m) is the high point of the trail but is not a place to stop; this area is threatened by rockfall and signs encourage you not to linger. Beyond this section the trail becomes easier, except for the odd exposed part. There are many places to sit and enjoy the views of the Mattertal. Up above are glaciers and peaks that can only be guessed at from the trail below.

A suspension bridge crosses the torrent gushing down from the Hochberggletscher and a sign advises no more than five people should be on the bridge at once. The void below suggests that this is probably good advice.

Another hour's walk and the **Europahütte** (2220m) is a welcome sight.

> This wooden building was newly constructed for the opening of the Europaweg and has a wonderful **terrace** facing over the Mattertal to the Weisshorn. This is the place to get out the binoculars and become intimately acquainted with the exquisitely sculpted North Face of this peak. At 4506m the Weisshorn is the second highest peak entirely in Switzerland, and there is no easy route to the summit.

This onward section has not been checked by the author since 2007 due to constant re-routing and closure of different sections.

◄ From here on the trail is more equipped with tunnels and cables than the earlier part. Soon after the hut there is a path down to Randa and a picnic table. A short descent leads to a tunnel cut through the rock – it helps if you find the light switch at the entrance, and in typical Swiss fashion this is solar powered. A bridge crosses another deep ravine before an improbable hillside is traversed, protected by rope railings.

As the path drops you pass another descent to Randa, with good views of the landslide.

In April and May 1991 there were several **land-slides** on the westerly hillside above Randa. The biggest one blocked the railway line, the road and the river, and the military were brought in to build a temporary pontoon bridge to evacuate people stranded in the upper Mattertal. Miraculously no one was hurt.

We are nearing the end of the exposed slopes of the Europaweg but a final section must be crossed – a sign warns of rockfall and the path is protected by a platform, then two tunnels. After this the terrain becomes gentler and enters forest of larch and Arolla pine. The Weisshorn now cedes its dominant position and the Matterhorn takes over. This makes the ascent to Täschalp more palatable, and before you know it you'll be coming into the delightful hamlet of **Ottovan** (2214m) which can also be reached by road from the valley.

Views from Ottovan are superb, with a background of the Täschhorn. There is a church and a café called the **Europaweghütte**. This is a lovely place to enjoy lunch, and if you have decided to take three days over this stage this is the place to stay.

Täschalp marks the end of the 'Alpine' nature of the Tour of Monte Rosa, and the final part of the trek follows pastoral tracks through forest and hamlets of wooden chalets. Monte Rosa stays hidden, although a look at the map shows it is not far away. The other Zermatt peaks take centre stage from here as you stroll onwards around the hillside heading for **Tufteren** (2215m).

A café here begs a last stop before you have to decide which way to take to reach **Zermatt**. Most people will want to complete the journey on foot, so take a wide track which goes past the cable car at Patrullarve and down through Tiefenmatten, arriving in town just over the river from the church. Alternatively the Sunnegga lift can be reached by following a wide track around the hillside.

FIGHTING COWS

Throughout the summer farmers organise 'Combat des Reines' to pit their best black Hérens cows against those owned by farmers in neighbouring valleys

While trekking in the Alps you are almost certain to see many different breeds of cows. They are all beautiful, and should not be feared. When you go past try not to scare them with your trekking poles. Although in general it is wise to keep a safe distance from their rear ends, it's worth taking the time to say hello and, if they want to, let them lick your hand – they like anything salty.

One particular type of cow will doubtless draw your attention. This is the dark brown or black Hérens cow, which is a race apart. This breed is very hardy and muscular and has a natural fighting tendency – not towards humans, but towards each other. The females will fight for dominance of the herd. They do not hurt each other – it's more a matter of intimidation – but the winner is the one who holds out the longest without backing off. This cow will then lead the herd for the season, and generally wears the biggest bell.

The local farmers hold regular contests between their cows, the Combat des Reines, where each farmer presents his bravest cow and they have a stand-off. Such events are worth going to if you happen to be around at the time, as they are seen as both a celebration of these fabulous animals and an excuse for a party.

However, as they say in France, 'Cows are made to sit and watch the trains' – and that's what most cows will do most of the time.

STAGE 8A

Grächen to Zermatt – valley route

Start	Grächen (1619m)
Finish	Zermatt (1600m)
Distance	22km
Total ascent	479m
Total descent	505m
Time	5½–6hrs
Maps	1:50,000 Carte Nationale de la Suisse 5006 Matterhorn Mischabel; 1:25,000 Carte Nationale de la Suisse 1328 Randa, 1308 St Niklaus
Access	To start: Grächen is reached from the Mattertal by bus from St Niklaus. To finish: Train from Visp; bus and road access to Täsch, then train to Zermatt.
Accommodation	Hotels at St Niklaus, Mattsand, Herbriggen, Randa, Täsch and Zermatt
Facilities	St Niklaus and Zermatt have everything you could ever need. The odd café is passed en route, notably near the train stations. Täsch is a bustling small town.

Although there are no high passes, no summits and no breathtaking belvederes (bar the very last section into Zermatt) this walk has a lot going for it, as well as being a safe option that is feasible in any weather. The walk down from Grächen is pretty and easy to follow, St Niklaus is worth a visit and there are many historic chalets and barns to admire all the way along the valley, some dating from an era when these villages were cut off from the rest of the world for at least six months of the year. There was no proper road up to Zermatt until 1862 and the year-round railway only came into existence in 1930. And, finally, you have a view of the mighty Matterhorn to enjoy before the northern fringes of Zermatt swallow you up.

From **Grächen** the trail to St Niklaus is well signposted and the way takes small roads and footpaths, often crossing the main access road to Grächen and passing lots of

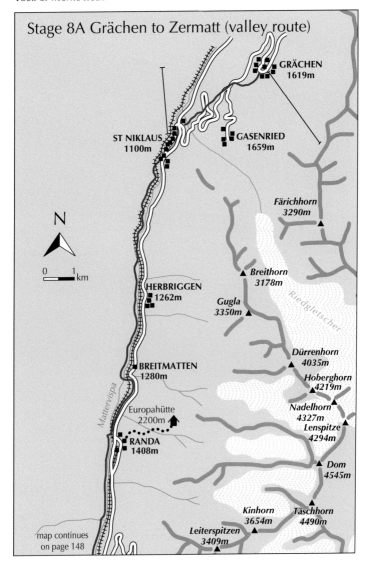

Stage 8A Grächen to Zermatt (valley route)

GRÄCHEN
1619m

ST NIKLAUS
1100m

GASENRIED
1659m

Färichhorn
3290m

N

0   1 km

Breithorn
3178m

HERBRIGGEN
1262m

Gugla
3350m

Riedgletscher

BREITMATTEN
1280m

Dürrenhorn
4035m

Hoberghorn
4219m

Nadelhorn
4327m

Europahütte
2200m

Lenspitze
4294m

RANDA
1408m

Mattervispa

Dom
4545m

Kinhorn
3654m

Täschhorn
4490m

Leiterspitzen
3409m

map continues
on page 148

146

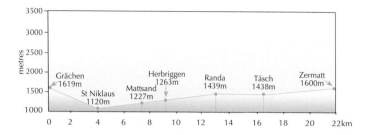

pretty chalets and well-tended gardens and vegetable plots. You reach the valley at Eye (also written Eie on some maps) and cross the river to climb up to **St Niklaus**. ▸

Take time to visit the fine onion-dome church.

Once in the village, cross the village square below St Niklaus railway station and bear right, then left down a narrow street to the old main road. Turn right and walk up-valley almost to the outskirts of the village (about 400m), where you break to the right on a minor road beside Restaurant zum Frävler.

> The way now follows what is apparently the **'old' road** through the valley, bringing you alongside the railway line and passing some typical old Valaisian houses, as well as more modern buildings based on traditional architectural styles. You'll be following the Zermatt Marathon markers as this wonderful mountain race begins in St Niklaus and Zermatt marks the halfway stage.

After a short while, you come to a group of old buildings and a small chapel; this is Ze Schwidernu (1163m). A few minutes later, as you cross the Blattbach stream which pours from the right, the Topali Hut can be seen as a silver box perched on a cliff 1400m above. Not long after, you arrive in the hamlet of Mattsand.

Still on the old road cross back over the railway line and the river beyond to gain a fine view of the Breithorn up-valley. The road now skirts a large settlement reservoir,

147

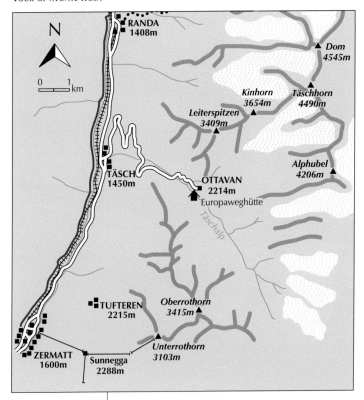

and when the tarmac road bears left round the southern end, go directly ahead on a continuing track. About a minute along this track pass a small picnic area on the left, and on the right a view up to a series of cascades pouring through the Tummigbach gorge. Shortly after this emerge from a wooded area to open meadows and old haybarns, the village of **Herbriggen** across the river, and another lovely view of the Breithorn.

At the far end of the meadow the track forks, with the left branch crossing the river to Herbriggen. Do not cross but instead continue along the valley on the right-hand side of the Mattervispa river. Eventually you'll reach a footbridge crossing the river to Herbriggen station. Again, do not cross, but remain on the west side of the river on a footpath signed to Randa, Täsch and Zermatt.

The path briefly accompanies the Mattervispa, past Breitmatten, then climbs among trees and forks. Keep ahead over a footbridge and contour briefly alongside an irrigation channel before climbing again, twisting uphill through mixed woodland. Having gained a high point, you then descend to the river and cross by footbridge. Go up a slope for a few paces, then bear right on a track signed to Randa.

> Just ahead can be seen the results of a huge **avalanche of rock** which exploded down the hillside in April and May 1991, destroying the road and railway line and causing the river to flood above Randa. Miraculously no-one was injured.

From here the track continues to follow the river upstream, then brings you to a service road by a bridge. Walk up the road. Screened from the river by a line of larch trees, the road rises gently. When it forks continue ahead, but when you reach some hay barns leave the road for a track cutting ahead to the right, with views now of the mighty Weisshorn summit.

A short distance along the track come to a road by a bridge on the outskirts of **Randa**. Cross the bridge and turn left on a riverside footpath which brings you to another junction soon after. Remain on the tree-lined riverside path, which after a while rises through forest, then descends again to the river and forks. Cross the river to another service road, recross the river once more, then continue on the riverside path. This goes up a brief slope, passes a shrine and leads to the Matterhorn Golf Course.

Skirt the right-hand side of the golf course, partly weaving through woodland, and eventually come to a group of buildings and a track. The track winds round a large building, continues a short distance along the valley, then twists left to cross a side stream. Turn left on the

Old wooden barns near Randa

continuing track, which soon curves to the right and goes alongside a man-made lake, at the far end of which you come to a large car park.

Cross the car park to an access road and resume alongside the Mattervispa river, soon passing a picnic area with a water supply on the right. You'll soon come to Camping Alphubel opposite **Täsch**. A bridge crosses the river to the village, but you only need to go into the village if you want accommodation there or if the cafés are calling.

> **Täsch** is a bustling little place and also home to several huge car parks. All but local Zermatt residents have to leave their vehicles here.

The route continues on the west bank of the river, past the campsite. A group of ancient larch barns marks the start of the final ascent up to Zermatt. Bear right on a path which climbs among larch and spruce, giving welcome shade on hot summer afternoons. This last section of the route is a lovely and quite popular walk, and you're likely to meet families and locals enjoying the woodland. The path is varied and short climbs are interspersed with flat sections.

Eventually, just after a couple of zigzags, you'll reach a bench; the Zermatt suburbs are below and ahead is… the Matterhorn!

> This is not the best view of the Matterhorn – that's to be had from the church in town – but nevertheless it's an important view and for that reason alone you should celebrate at this point. Or at least breathe a huge sigh of relief – the journey is almost over!
>
> Sadly this northern end of **Zermatt** is a permanent construction site as the new apartment blocks push edges of town ever further outwards. It's also the home of all the dirty reality of a thriving tourist centre – rubbish bins and vehicles bringing supplies in – and also the dredging of silt from the river. However, it's fun to pass the Air Zermatt hangar and see the helicopters landing and taking off.

Just beyond the Air Zermatt heli-pad a concrete path goes down left, and deposits you at the train station. Cross the railway line and go and embrace the wonderful craziness of Zermatt. Your journey is complete – time to reflect on this amazing mountain experience.

APPENDIX A
Route summary table

Stage no	Start and Finish	Distance	Time	Ascent	Descent	Page
1	Zermatt to Theodulpass	11km	6–7hrs	1701m	0m	68
2	Theodulpass to Resy *to alternative finish St Jacques*	14km *14.5km*	5hrs *5hrs*	351m *151m*	1580m *1779m*	76
3	Resy to Gabiet *from alternative start St Jacques*	10km *10.5km*	5hrs 30mins–6hrs *6–6hrs 30mins*	1119m *1319m*	850m *850m*	86
3A	St Jacques to Gabiet via Colle di Pinter	20km	12hrs	1805m	1152m	94
4	Gabiet to Alagna *to alternative finish Rifugio Pastore*	11.5km *15.5km*	4½hrs *6hrs*	546m *941m*	1748m *1748m*	100
5	Alagna to Macugnaga *from alternative start Rifugio Pastore*	20km *16km*	9–10hrs *8+hrs*	1649m *1254m*	1512m *1512m*	110
6	Macugnaga to Saas Fee	20km	11hrs	1536m	1180	117
7	Saas Fee to Grächen	16km	8hrs	700m	900m	127
8	Grächen to Zermatt (Europaweg)	31km	10–11hrs	1300m	1200m	135
8A	Grächen to Zermatt (valley route)	22km	5½–6hrs	479m	505m	145

APPENDIX B

Summits of the Monte Rosa massif

The massif of Monte Rosa is made of crystalline and metamorphic rocks, such as marble and quartz, and its great ridge of main peaks runs for about 30km between Italy and Switzerland forming, more or less, the Swiss-Italian border. The range culminates in the Dufourspitze (Punta Dufour) (4634m).

The group includes 34 main peaks above 3000m and 22 peaks higher than 4000m; 13 or 14 of these are designated independent 4000m summits by those looking to climb all the summits over this height in the Alps. They are marked with an asterisk below (the jury still seems to be out on Punta Giordani). Those marked with two asterisks are the actual summits of Monte Rosa.

THE 4000M PEAKS

  ** Dufourspitze (4634m) (Punta Dufour, Valais, Switzerland)
  ** Nordend (4609m) (Piedmont, Italy)
  ** Punta Zumstein (4563m) (Zumsteinspitze, Valle d'Aosta, Italy)
  ** Punta Gnifetti (4556m) (Signalkuppe, Piedmont, Italy)
   * Punta Lys East (4527m) (Liskamm East, Valle d'Aosta, Italy)
     Punta Lys West (4479m) (Liskamm West, Valle d'Aosta, Italy)
  ** Punta Parrot (4436m) (Parrotspitze, Piedmont, Italy)
  ** Punta Ludwig (4341m) (Ludwigshohe, Valle d'Aosta, Italy)
  ** Corno Nero (4322m) (Schwarzhorn, Piedmont, Italy)
     Naso della Lyskamm (4272m) (Liskammnase, Valle d'Aosta, Italy)
   * Castor (4228m) (Castore, Valais, Switzerland)
  ** Piramide Vincent (4215m) (Valle d'Aosta, Italy)
     Roccia della Scoperta (4178m) (Entdeckungsfels, Valle d'Aosta, Italy)
  ** Punta Balm (4167m) (Balmenhorn, Piedmont, Italy)
   * Breithorn West (4164m) (Valle d'Aosta, Italy)
     Breithorn Mid (4159m) (Valle d'Aosta, Italy)
     Breithorn East (4139m) (Valle d'Aosta, Italy)
     Breithomzwillinge East (4106m) (Valais, Switzerland)
     Felikhorn (4093m) (Punta Felik, Valais, Switzerland)
   * Pollux (4092m) (Polluce, Valais, Switzerland)
     Roccia Nera (4075m) (Piedmont, Italy
 (**)Punta Giordani (4046m) (Piedmont, Italy)

MAIN PEAKS SEEN FROM THE TOUR

The Tour of Monte Rosa gives the opportunity to discover a whole massif, spanning two countries. Time and again your eyes will be drawn to the fabulous high mountains all around, both close at hand and far away. Some will be glimpsed only briefly, others will become regulars on your journey. It's interesting to know a little about some of the main players.

Weisshorn (4505m)

The Weisshorn is the second-highest summit solely in Switzerland, and was apparently named by the people of St Niklaus for the luminosity of its North Face. You will come to know its North and East Face well when you walk the Europaweg from Grächen to Zermatt. It was first ascended by Irishman John Tyndall in 1861, with Guides JJ Bennen and U Wenger. Tyndall was a contender for the first ascent of the Matterhorn, and one of the ridge pinnacles on that peak is named after him. He became famous for discovering that the sky is blue because of the diffusion of light.

There are no easy routes up the Weisshorn. The beauty and purity of this pyramidal summit has made the Weisshorn one of the most sought-after 4000m peaks in the Alps. The mountain has extra kudos as there is no road or lift to help reduce the ascent; even the Normal Route, the East Ridge, requires a long ascent from and descent to the valley.

Dom (4545m)

This is the highest peak entirely in Switzerland, and stands proud on the east side of the Mattertal. Its name has variously been reported to come from that of Canon (Domherr) Berchthold who was the first to survey the Valais canton, or to have been given by him and to mean Deo Optimo Maximo (God is good and big). Whichever version is true, there's no doubt that the Dom has a size and magnificence that reach heavenly proportions. Nevertheless, its ascent by the North Face presents no real difficulties, being a huge glaciated slope which is popular in summer and winter alike as the Normal Route up the mountain. It was first ascended in 1858 by Rev. JL Davies with Guides J Zum Taugwald, J Kronig and J Schwarzen. They left Randa at 2am, reached the summit at 11am, and returned to Randa at 4.20pm to then walk up to Zermatt for dinner.

Breithorn (4164m)

'Wide mountain' would be the literal translation of Breithorn and the name fits this summit well – the Breithorn stretches well over 2km from its main western summit to the eastern one. Its huge bulk towers above Zermatt and can be seen when coming up the Mattertal well before the Matterhorn deigns to show itself. The Breithorn is not the highest peak in the area but it must be the most climbed due to its accessibility from the Klein Matterhorn lift and the relative ease of ascent from the south side. Richard Goedeke is not really impressed with the development of this area as he states 'for those who relish the beauty and remoteness of an unspoiled mountain the ascent of the last few hundred metres of the most climbed 4000er... will be more masochism than pleasure'. While it's true that this peak is 'open to all', that doesn't alter the fact that the views from the summit are splendid and you still have to climb for three hours at around 4000m.

This is the most westerly peak of the giants which rise up from the Gorner Glacier, and it has four summits: the westerly high point, the central summit (4159m), the eastern summit (4139m), and Roccia Nera (4075m) which – as its name suggests – is a rocky summit above the Schwarztor col which separates it from Pollux.

The Breithorn was first climbed by the South Face route in 1813 (when it was somewhat more of an endeavour without the aid of lifts) by H Maynard, JM Couttet, Jean Gras, and JB and JJ Erin.

Castor (4228m)/Pollux (4092m)

Named either after the sons of the Goddess Leda, heroes of Greek mythology, or a constellation, these are the Zwillinge (twins) seen as two small summits surrounded as they are by giants. They are between the huge mountain masses of the Breithorn and Liskamm. Castor is the south-easterly and higher twin and appears as a rounded white summit, whereas Pollux is rockier. These peaks are often climbed together in a day, both in winter and summer, and can be incorporated into a multi-day glaciated traverse of the Zermatt frontier peaks.

They are easy to identify when you have views of the whole range from the Breithorn to Liskamm, such as from Gornergrat. They are also, of course, visible from the Breithorn and the descent to Zermatt.

Liskamm (4527m)

Liskamm can boast a mighty 5km-long ridge, an arête notorious for its cornices (often double-sided), and a traverse of the mountain is only for those with stable feet and steady nerves. It has two summits, the east of which rises 50m higher than the west, which is about a kilometre away. Its original name of Silberbast ('silver saddle' in local dialect) would therefore seem appropriate.

The peak was first ascended in 1861, the 1860s being a time of great activity in these mountains. The first ascent party was a huge team of six Swiss Guides and eight British clients, and they took a route up the East Ridge. The peak was first traversed by Guides J Anderegg and F Biner with L Stephen and E Buxton in 1864. The first disaster on the mountain occurred in 1877 when a party fell to their deaths when a cornice broke. This was the start of this mountain's dark history, leading to the reputation it has today. As Oscar Erich Meyer put it, those who have died 'did not die at its foot, on its walls or on its ridges, but were cast from the crest into the depths. All at once, all whom the rope had bound together. For thus are cornices. Day after day the wind kneads and shapes them...and it is man who, in deadly bond with his companions, tips the scales. Thus the Liskamm kills. It gives no warnings, it strikes like lightening.'

So, probably a peak best enjoyed from afar – you'll get good views of it if you climb the Breithorn.

Weissmies (4023m)

This is the highest mountain in the northeastern Pennine Alps, to the east of the Saastal, and is without doubt one of the most appealing peaks in the region. It can be climbed by a relatively easy route and with a bit more effort and technique can be traversed from south to north, to give one of the best Alpine outings around.

First climbed by PJ Zurbriggen and JC Heuser via its southeast ridge in 1856, today the Normal Route is the Northwest Face, a glacier walk. This route has the advantage that the hut (Hohsaas) can be reached by cable car, making for a very easy first day.

The Weissmies is seen from the Höhenweg from Saas Fee to Grächen (although you do need to look backwards for most of the time to see it).

Matterhorn (4478m)

Zermatt and Breuil-Cervinia are dominated by the imposing pyramid of the Matterhorn (Monte Cervino in Italian),

one of the most exceptional summits in the world. When seen from the Swiss side it is often regarded as the classic peak – a perfect pyramid –and is used extensively for all sorts of publicity, advertising and inspiration.

The Matterhorn has no easy route to the summit, and was one of the last major peaks in the Alps to be climbed. By the mid-19th century the first ascent of the Matterhorn was a much sought-after goal. The two main candidates were JA Carrel from Breuil, and England's prodigious alpinist Edward Whymper. Several attempts had been made, all resulting in retreat, but in mid-July 1865 both men felt confident they could reach the summit.

Whymper expected to undertake the climb accompanied by Carrel, but arriving in Breuil found that Carrel had already assembled his own team and was en route. Hurrying back to Zermatt Whymper knew he could be pipped at the post if he didn't get moving. His choice of partners was limited to those who were free at that moment. Along with Michel Croz, his faithful Chamonix Guide, Whymper teamed up with a motley assortment of more or less experienced climbers: Lord Francis Douglas, Swiss Guides Peter Taugwalder and his son, Reverend Charles Hudson and Douglas Hadow. They set off immediately, keenly aware of Carrel's head start.

They took the Northeast Ridge of the mountain known as the Hörnli, and made quick progress. After a final steeper climb they succeeded in their quest, and looking down from the summit could see Carrel's team some way below on the Italian Ridge. Allegedly Whymper and team knocked rocks down to signify their presence, making sure there was no doubt they had got there first. Understandably Carrel was just a touch miffed and he gave up for the day, even though he had almost made the first ascent of the Southwest Ridge from Italy.

However, the Zermatt team had yet to get down. Slopes always feel much steeper on descent, and the Hörnli ridge of the Matterhorn is no exception. Factor in the inexperience of some team members, the inevitable fatigue and perhaps lack of concentration following such a momentous

ascent, and it's hardly surprising that Hadow slipped. The tragedy is that he took with him Croz, Hudson and Douglas. The slender hemp rope, loaded well beyond its limit by the enormous impact of several bodies sliding into space, broke, leaving the Taudwalders and Whymper to descend to Zermatt to break the tragic news.

Carrel climbed his Italian Ridge three days later.

Nowadays the Matterhorn is the goal of many alpinists and a sunny summer's day will see hoards of people on the summit, many ascending by one of the ridges described above. Nevertheless it still remains a summit to be reckoned with, and since the first ascent there have been hundreds of deaths on its steep slopes.

Looking across to the summits of Liskamm during the ascent of Monte Rosa

APPENDIX C
Accommodation

Stage 1
Zermatt

Hotels

Gandegghütte
tel: 079 607 88 68
richard@pratoborni.ch

Testa Grigia – Rifugio Guide del
Cervino
tel: 0166 948369
info@rifugioguidedelcervino.com

Theodulhütte
tel: 0166 949400

Stage 2
Breuil-Cervinia

Hotels

Rifugio Guide di Frachey
tel: 0125 307468
info@rifugioguidefrachey.com

Rifugio GB Ferraro
tel: 0125 307612
mail@rifugioferraro.com

St Jacques
Hotels

Stage 3

Rifugio Gabiet
tel: 0125 366258
info@rifugiogabiet.it

Albergo del Ponte
tel: 0125 328736
info@albergodelponte.com

Gressoney la Trinité/Gressoney St Jean

Hotels

Rifugio Alpenzu
tel: 338 2562229

Orestes Hütte
tel: 0125 1925 484
info@oresteshuette.eu

Stage 4
Alagna

Hotels

Rifugio Pastore
tel: 0163 91220
info@rifugiopastore.it

Rifugio Zar Senni, Otro
tel: 331 7383271
zar.senni@libero.it

Rifugio Città di Mortara (Grande Halte)
tel: 348 8752203
info@grandehalte.it

Stage 5

Macugnaga

Hotels

Stage 6

Rifugio Oberto Maroli
tel: 0324 65544
valcot.rifugio@gmail.com

Saastal

Hotels

Saas Fee

Hotels

Stage 7

Grächen/Gasenreid

Hotels

Stage 8

Europahütte
tel: 027 967 8247
europahuette@sunrise.ch

Ottovan Täschalp Europaweghütte
tel: 027 967 2301
europaweg2200@gmail.com

Täsch

Hotels

Randa

Hotels

Zermatt

Hotels

APPENDIX D
Useful contacts

All phone numbers are noted in the form used when phoning from within the respective country. When phoning from elsewhere add the country code and change the numbers accordingly: to call a Swiss number from outside Switzerland dial the international code (in Europe usually 00) followed by the country code 41, then drop the first zero of the number; to call an Italian number from outside Italy dial the international code followed by the country code 39, then the Italian number in its entirety, keeping the zero.

Tourist offices

Switzerland
Zermatt
tel: 027 966 8100
info@zermatt.ch

Täsch
tel: 027 967 1689
info@taesch.ch

Randa
tel: 027 967 1677
tourismus@randa.ch

Grächen
tel: 027 955 6060
info@graechen.ch

Saas Fee
tel: 027 958 18 58
to@saas-fee.ch

Saas Grund
tel: 027 957 1855
info@saas-grund.ch

Saas Almagell
tel: 027 957 1888
info@saas-almagell.ch

Italy
Aosta region
www.regione.vda.it
www.lovevda.it

Breuil-Cervinia
tel: 0166 949136
cervinia@turismo.vda.it

Alagna
tel: 0163 922988
infoalagna@atlvalsesiavercelli.it

Gressoney la Trinité/Gressoney St Jean
tel: 0125 366143
gressoneylatrinite@turismo.vda.it

Macugnaga
tel: 0324 65119
iat@comune.macugnaga.vb.it

Guides offices
Zermatt
tel: 027 966 2460
alpincenter@zermatt.ch

Saas Fee
tel: 027 957 4464
info@saasfeeguides.ch

Breuil-Cervinia (Italy)
tel: 0166 948169
info@guidedelcervino.com

Route information
Tour of Monte Rosa official website
www.tmr-matterhorn.ch

Europaweg official website
www.europaweg.ch

Travel and transport
British Airways
tel: 0844 493 0787
www.britishairways.com

Easyjet
tel: 0820 420315
www.easyjet.com

Swiss International
tel: 0848 700700
www.swiss.com

Aer Lingus (fly to Geneva)
tel: 0818 365000
www.aerlingus.com

Zurich airport
tel: 043 816 2211
www.zurich-airport.com

Geneva airport
tel: 022 717 7111
www.gva.ch

Turin airport
tel: 011 5676361
www.aeroportoditorino.it

Milan Malpensa
tel: 02 232323
www.milanomalpensa-airport.com

Eurolines (coach travel)
tel: 08717 818178
www.eurolines.com

SBB (Swiss Rail)
www.sbb.ch

Maps
The Map Shop
Tel: 01684 593146
themapshop@btinternet.com
www.themapshop.co.uk

Stanfords
Tel: 020 7836 1321
sales@stanfords.co.uk
www.stanfords.co.uk

Weather information
www.weatheronline.co.uk
Provides long-term forecasts for Europe

Swiss Alps
www.meteosuisse.ch
www.zermatt.com
General information
www.sac-cas.ch
Swiss Alpine Club site, providing lots of useful links
By phone: 162 Press 1 when told to then # (*diaz*) when told to.

Italian Alps
www.regione.vda.it
General information and weather forecasts
www.lovevda.it
General information and weather forecasts
By phone (Aosta region):
0165 44113
Local weather forecasts are usually posted outside tourist offices.

APPENDIX E
Glossary of useful terms

alpage	summer farm used in the process of transhumance (see below).
bisse	man-made waterway or irrigation channel
col/colle	pass or a saddle; in German usually "joch"; in Italian "colle" or "bocca"
cwm/corrie/ combe	basin surrounded on three sides by hills or mountains either steep sided or more gently rounded. Often holds a lake, with a stream flowing out of the unenclosed side down into the valley
tal	valley, as in Mattertal, Saastal and so on
transhumance	system of farming in the Alps whereby animals are taken to graze the higher meadows during the summer months

Weather

German	English	French	Italian
wetter	weather	*temps*	*tempo*
vorhersage (wetter)	forecast	*prévision*	*bolletino*
heiss	hot	*chaud*	*caldo*
kalt	cold	*froid*	*freddo*
sonnig	sunny	*ensoleillé*	*soleggiato*
regnerisch	rainy	*pluvieux*	*piovos*
windig	windy	*venteux*	*ventoso*
bewölkt	cloudy	*nuageux*	*nuvoloso*
neblig	foggy	*brouillard*	*nebbioso*
stürmisch	stormy	*orageux*	*temporalesco*
schneereich	snowy	*enneigé*	*nevoso*
temperatur	temperature	*température*	*temperatura*
veränderlich verschneit	changeable	*variable*	*variabile*
donner	thunder	*tonnère*	*tuono*
blitz	lightning	*éclair*	*fulmine*

German	English	French	Italian
bö, windstoss	gusts/gales	*rafales*	*raffiche di vento*
verlieren der sicht	white out	*jour blanc*	*luce abbacinante*
eis	ice	*glace*	*ghiaccio*
glatteis	verglace	*verglas*	*ghiaccio vivo, verglace*
hagel	hall	*grêle*	*grandine*
lawine	avalanche	*avalanche*	*valanga*
eisig, eiskalt	freezing	*glacial*	*congelamento*
sternklar	starry	*étoillé*	*stellato*

Emergency

German	English	French	Italian
hilfe	help!	*au secours!*	*aiuto!*
unfall	accident	*accident*	*incidente*
notfall	emergency	*urgence*	*emergenza*
stop	stop!	*halte*	*stop (alt)*
schnell	quick	*vite*	*presto*
achtung	be careful!	*faites attention*	*attenzione*
retten, rettung	rescue	*secours*	*soccorso*
hubschrauber	helicopter	*hélicoptère*	*elicottero*
ambulanz	ambulance	*ambulance*	*ambulanza*
spital	hospital	*hôpital*	*ospedale*
doktor, arzt	doctor	*medecin/ docteur dottore*	*medico*
nottelefon	SOS telephone	*téléphone d'urgence*	*telefono di soccorso*
schlaganfall	stroke	*hémiplégie*	*attacco*
armbruch	broken arm/leg	*bras/jambe cassé(e)*	*braccio rotto, gamba rotta*
asthmaanfall	asthma attack	*crise d'asthma*	*attacco d'asma*

APPENDIX F

Glacier travel and
crevasse rescue techniques

Adapted from *Snowshoeing: Mont Blanc and the Western Alps* by Hilary Sharp. The principal hazard of glacier travel is that of hidden crevasses. On a dry glacier (that is, a glacier not covered with snow) crevasses are obvious and therefore pose few problems. However, on a wet (snow-covered) glacier what lurks beneath the surface presents a very real danger.

Travel on a wet glacier, therefore, is always undertaken roped together – even if there is a good track and good visibility. Roping up wrongly and/or using the rope incorrectly can make any crevasse incident worse. It is therefore essential to adopt correct practice and to keep to certain guidelines. This guide is not intended as an instruction manual, and what follows is more of a reminder. Glacier travel and crevasse rescue techniques must be learnt and practised, either on a specialised course or from an experienced mountaineer or a professional.

Each participant should be equipped with the minimum of an ice axe, a harness and screwgate krab, an ice screw, a 120cm sling, three prussik loops, a pulley and three spare karabiners. The party should have a dynamic rope, the minimum diameter of which should be 8mm, although in practice a larger diameter is more user-friendly when it comes to handling in a crevasse rescue situation. It is not necessary to have a designated single rope of 10 or 11mm if only pure glacier travel is envisaged. The minimum length should be about 30m for two people. For larger numbers a longer rope or two ropes should be used.

We will look at glacier travel for a party of two people. The walkers should be roped together with about 10m of rope between them (see Figure 1). To do this each should tie into the ends of the rope and take an equal number of coils around their shoulders until the middle 10m is left. The coils are tied off

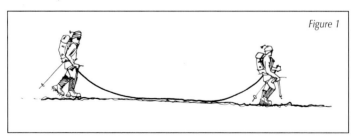

Figure 1

Figure 2

One trekking pole should be stowed away on the rucksack leaving that hand free for the ice axe. The axe *must* be instantly available for arresting a fall, not attached to the back of the rucksack. It should be carried by the head, with the shaft downwards like a walking stick, in the uphill hand whenever appropriate.

Two further refinements of this basic system are the pre-attachment of prussik loops to the rope and the tying of knots in the rope at intervals along the 10m. The theory behind the latter method is that in the event of a crevasse fall the rope will cut into the snow lip and the knot will jam into the snow, thus arresting the fall. The downside of this system is that if the snow is very soft the knot will pass right through the snow and will hinder the subsequent rescue.

by passing a bight of rope around them and tying an overhand knot around the rope that leads between the walkers. This leaves a loop, which can be clipped back into the harness with the screwgate karabiner.

When walking the rope should be kept reasonably tight – so that the middle 5–6m glide along the snow. If this tension is maintained, not only will the rope be kept away from sharp crampons, it also avoids the dangerous practice of holding the rope up in your hand, the result of which can be a serious shoulder injury in the event of a crevasse fall. Under no circumstances should coils be carried in the hand on a wet glacier.

It is worth considering putting the lightest person at the front as disparity in weight is an important factor, but bear in mind that it's not always the first person to cross that breaks a fragile snow bridge.

Although both members of the party should be vigilant at all times on a glacier, some particularly crevassed areas will obviously be more dangerous than others. This information should be passed back from the leader so that the second person can prepare himself and tighten the rope further.

The first reaction to one of the walkers falling into a crevasse can determine success or failure. If the other person is pulled flat on his face then arresting the fall becomes very difficult. The ideal reaction is to jerk backwards and adopt a semi-sitting position, with the shaft of the axe plunged into the snow (see Figure 2).

Before doing anything else the rescuer should:

- Shout to try to make contact with the victim – it may well be that by lowering him slightly he will be able to walk out of the crevasse on the other side.

- Look around for other people. A group of 4 or 5 people will be able to use brute force to pull the

victim up or, at worst, help in the following stages of the rescue.

- Ascertain whether it's possible for the victim to ascend the rope using his prussik loops, assuming he knows how to do this.

The basic belay for crevasse rescue in snow is the horizontally buried ice axe (if the snow isn't deep enough then this is where the ice screw comes in). A slot must first be cut, using the axe, at right angles to the pull of the rope and as deep as possible. It should be the length of the axe and the forward wall should be slightly incut to avoid the axe being pulled out. A second slot, this time in line with the pull, should be cut, thus forming a T. It must be the same depth as the first slot and should rise to the surface at as shallow an angle as possible (see Figure 3). Doing this is not easy and is further hindered by the coils around the rescuer's shoulders. These can be slipped over the head to leave the upper body free.

When the slot is prepared, lark's foot or clove hitch a sling around the axe at approximately two thirds of the way up the shaft towards the head (this is to provide an equal bearing surface to prevent the axe from pivoting). The axe is pushed horizontally into the 'tee' of the slot and the sling laid into the right-angle slot. A krab is clipped to

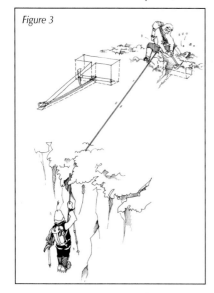

Figure 3

Figure 4

Figure 5

the sling. A prussik loop is tied in an autobloc/French prussik around the tight rope as close as possible to the krab and then clipped to this. Now the prussik is pushed forward as tight as possible and the rescuer should slide forward gently to transfer the victim's weight to the autobloc. The shoulder coils can be undone and removed methodically and finally the rope on the slack side of the autobloc should be clipped through the krab. This is now referred to as a clutch.

For the rescuer to operate in safety he must be attached to the belay. The easiest way to do this is to attach himself temporarily to the belay with one prussik, then untie from the end of the rope and clip this to the belay. He should then attach himself to the rope via an Italian hitch into the screwgate krab on his harness. He must carefully approach the edge of the crevasse, paying out the rope through the hitch (effectively abseiling , although not necessarily weighting the belay). Having ascertained that the victim needs pulling out, the edge of the crevasse must be prepared by pushing trekking poles under the rope as near to the edge as possible to prevent further cutting into the lip. The remaining snow lip can be broken away. The victim must now be told to clip his ice axe and pole to his harness (see Figure 4).

If the rope hasn't bitten too far into the lip or the weight/strength difference of the walkers isn't to the rescuer's disadvantage, it might be possible to lift the victim using a 3:1 pulley system, sometimes referred to as a Z pulley. A second prussik loop is tied onto the taut rope close to the poles at the lip and a krab and pulley clipped to it. The slack rope from the clutch can now be clipped through the pulley. Pulling the rope back towards the belay now gives a mechanical advantage of 3:1. (It is important to note that regardless of whether the 3:1 will provide enough mechanical advantage or not, it is also the first stage for the improved 6:1 system.) As the victim moves upwards the autobloc forming the clutch slackens and allows the rope to run through it. When the rescuer tires he can gently release the load and the clutch will reactivate and hold the victim's weight again. Similarly, when the pulley has been pulled up tight against the belay the clutch can be used to hold the victim while the pulley is slid back down the rope to start again (see Figure 5).

As noted above, hoisting using a 3:1 system is usually only possible if the victim is considerably lighter than the rescuer or if other rescuers are available so the next step is to quickly and easily convert your 3:1 into a 6:1.

The third prussik loop is tied onto the rope as it exits the pulley and the third krab is clipped to it. The other end of the rope – which up to now has protected the rescuer – can be clipped

Figure 6

through the third krab. Pulling on this results in a 6:1 system. The rescuer will have a fair amount of running around to do as for every 6m of rope he pulls in the victim will rise only 1m (see Figure 6).

Finally as the victim nears the lip he will have to try to extract the rope from where it has bitten in by pulling and bracing his feet against the wall of the crevasse. At the last moment the rescuer may be able to crawl forward to help the victim out.

APPENDIX G
Background reading

There are many books about the Alps, but the following are good to read and provide lots of useful information. There are also some books about associated places such as the Valle d'Aosta.

Zermatt Saga by Cicely Williams (Roten-Verlag, 1989) is an account of Zermatt from the year dot by the wife of the Bishop of the English Church in Zermatt in the 1960s. Mrs Williams spent time in Zermatt since childhood and is clearly in love with the place. While her description of life there in the present day is rather dated, her history is spot on, and the book gives an insight to what can only be described as a bygone age.

How the English made the Alps by Jim Ring (John Murray, 2000) is a broad account of the activities of English mountaineers throughout the Alps. Many first ascents of Alpine peaks were made by local Guides with English clients, and this book is an easy and interesting read.

The High Mountains of the Alps by Helmut Dumler and Willi Burkhardt (Diadem, 1994) is the bible for all those who dream of ascending these giants; the photos alone will provide more than enough inspiration.

Scrambles amongst the Alps by Edward Whymper (National Geographic, 2002) provides a first-hand account of the fateful first ascent of the Matterhorn, as well as many more detailed accounts of climbing during the 1860s.

Ulrich Inderbinen: As old as the century by Heidi Lanz and Liliane De Meester (Roten-Verlag, 1997) tells Ulrich Inderbinen's story of growing up and becoming a Guide in Zermatt.

Our Alpine Flora by the Swiss Alpine Club (SAC, 1989) will fund many hours of research in the evenings as you try to figure out what 'those flowers' are.

The Alpine 4000m Peaks by Richard Goedeke (Diadem, 1993) describes the 61 official 4000m peaks in the Alps by their Normal Routes. The bible for peak-baggers!

Trekking and Climbing in the Western Alps by Hilary Sharp (New Holland, 2002) includes a description of the Tour of Monte Rosa as well as the Normal Routes up several summits on the region, notably the Weissmies, the Allalinhorn, the Breithorn and Monte Rosa. Sadly out of print.

Trekking in the Alps edited by Kev Reynolds (Cicerone Press, 2011) includes a description of the Tour of Monte Rosa by Hilary Sharp as well as many other alpines treks by Cicerone authors.

The Valle d'Aosta and its Castles by Giorgio Giubelli (Co. Graf, 1996) is one of several similar books available in English recounting the history and culture of the Aosta region.

NOTES

NOTES

LISTING OF CICERONE GUIDES

BRITISH ISLES CHALLENGES, COLLECTIONS AND ACTIVITIES

The End to End Trail
The Mountains of England and Wales: 1&2
The National Trails
The Relative Hills of Britain
The Ridges of England, Wales and Ireland
The UK Trailwalker's Handbook
The UK's County Tops
Three Peaks, Ten Tors

UK CYCLING

20 Classic Sportive Rides
  South West England
  South East England
Border Country Cycle Routes
Cycling in the Cotswolds
Cycling in the Hebrides
Cycling in the Peak District
Cycling in the Yorkshire Dales
Cycling the Pennine Bridleway
Mountain Biking in the Lake District
Mountain Biking in the Yorkshire Dales
Mountain Biking on the North Downs
Mountain Biking on the South Downs
The C2C Cycle Route
The End to End Cycle Route
The Lancashire Cycleway

SCOTLAND

Backpacker's Britain
  Central and Southern Scottish Highlands
  Northern Scotland
Ben Nevis and Glen Coe
Great Mountain Days in Scotland
Not the West Highland Way
Scotland's Best Small Mountains
Scotland's Far West
Scotland's Mountain Ridges
Scrambles in Lochaber
The Ayrshire and Arran Coastal Paths
The Border Country
The Cape Wrath Trail
The Great Glen Way
The Isle of Mull
The Isle of Skye

The Pentland Hills
The Skye Trail
The Southern Upland Way
The Speyside Way
The West Highland Way
Walking Highland Perthshire
Walking in Scotland's Far North
Walking in the Angus Glens
Walking in the Cairngorms
Walking in the Ochils, Campsie Fells and Lomond Hills
Walking in the Southern Uplands
Walking in Torridon
Walking Loch Lomond and the Trossachs
Walking on Harris and Lewis
Walking on Jura, Islay and Colonsay
Walking on Rum and the Small Isles
Walking on the Isle of Arran
Walking on the Orkney and Shetland Isles
Walking on Uist and Barra
Walking the Corbetts
  1 South of the Great Glen
  2 North of the Great Glen
Walking the Galloway Hills
Walking the Lowther Hills
Walking the Munros
  1 Southern, Central and Western Highlands
  2 Northern Highlands and the Cairngorms
Winter Climbs Ben Nevis and Glen Coe
Winter Climbs in the Cairngorms
World Mountain Ranges: Scotland

NORTHERN ENGLAND TRAILS

A Northern Coast to Coast Walk
Hadrian's Wall Path
The Dales Way
The Pennine Way

NORTH EAST ENGLAND, YORKSHIRE DALES AND PENNINES

Great Mountain Days in the Pennines
Historic Walks in North Yorkshire
South Pennine Walks
St Oswald's Way and St Cuthbert's Way

The Cleveland Way and the Yorkshire Wolds Way
The North York Moors
The Reivers Way
The Teesdale Way
The Yorkshire Dales
  North and East
  South and West
Walking in County Durham
Walking in Northumberland
Walking in the North Pennines
Walks in Dales Country
Walks in the Yorkshire Dales
Walks on the North York Moors – Books 1 & 2

NORTH WEST ENGLAND AND THE ISLE OF MAN

Historic Walks in Cheshire
Isle of Man Coastal Path
The Isle of Man
The Lune Valley and Howgills
The Ribble Way
Walking in Cumbria's Eden Valley
Walking in Lancashire
Walking in the Forest of Bowland and Pendle
Walking on the West Pennine Moors
Walks in Lancashire Witch Country
Walks in Ribble Country
Walks in Silverdale and Arnside
Walks in the Forest of Bowland

LAKE DISTRICT

Coniston Copper Mines
Great Mountain Days in the Lake District
Lake District: High Fell Walks
Lake District: Low Level and Lake Walks
Lake District Winter Climbs
Lakeland Fellranger
  The Central Fells
  The Far-Eastern Fells
  The Mid-Western Fells
  The Near Eastern Fells
  The Northern Fells
  The North-Western Fells
  The Southern Fells
  The Western Fells
Roads and Tracks of the Lake District
Rocky Rambler's Wild Walks

For full information on all our
guides, books and eBooks,
visit our website:
www.cicerone.co.uk.

Walking – Trekking – Mountaineering – Climbing – Cycling

Over 40 years, Cicerone have built up an outstanding collection of 300 guides, inspiring all sorts of amazing adventures.

Every guide comes from extensive exploration and research by our expert authors, all with a passion for their subjects. They are frequently praised, endorsed and used by clubs, instructors and outdoor organisations.

All our titles can now be bought as **e-books** and many as iPad and Kindle files and we will continue to make all our guides available for these and many other devices.

Our website shows any **new information** we've received since a book was published. Please do let us know if you find anything has changed, so that we can pass on the latest details. On our **website** you'll also find some great ideas and lots of information, including sample chapters, contents lists, reviews, articles and a photo gallery.

It's easy to keep in touch with what's going on at Cicerone, by getting our monthly **free e-newsletter**, which is full of offers, competitions, up-to-date information and topical articles. You can subscribe on our home page and also follow us on **Facebook** and **Twitter**, as well as our **blog**.

Cicerone – the very best guides for exploring the world.

CICERONE

2 Police Square Milnthorpe Cumbria LA7 7PY
Tel: 015395 62069 info@cicerone.co.uk
www.cicerone.co.uk